Forget Camus

Forget Camus

Confronting the Humanist Myth

Oliver Gloag

VERSO

London • New York

English-language edition first published by Verso 2026
First published as *Oublier Camus*
© Fabrique 2023
© Oliver Gloag 2023, 2026

The manufacturer's authorized representative in the EU for product safety (GPSR)
is LOGOS EUROPE, 9 rue Nicolas Poussin, 17000, La Rochelle, France
Contact@logoseurope.eu

1 3 5 7 9 10 8 6 4 2

Verso
UK: 6 Meard Street, London W1F 0EG
US: 207 East 32nd Street, New York, NY 10016
versobooks.com

Verso is the imprint of New Left Books

ISBN-13: 978-1-83674-270-8
ISBN-13: 978-1-83674-273-9 (US EBK)
ISBN-13: 978-1-83674-271-5 (UK EBK)

British Library Cataloguing in Publication Data
A catalogue record for this book is available from the British Library

Library of Congress Cataloging-in-Publication Data
A catalog record for this book is available from the Library of Congress

Typeset in Sabon by MJ & N Gavan, Truro, Cornwall
Printed and bound by CPI Group (UK) Ltd, Croydon CR0 4YY

To
Elaine Mokhtefi
'on the same side of history and sensitivity'
and in memory of
Fredric Jameson, Dorothea von Moltke and Julian Gloag

Contents

Foreword

On n'abdique pas l'honneur d'être une cible.[1]
– Edmond Rostand, *Cyrano de Bergerac*

Umberto Eco wrote that a title should confuse the reader; three centuries earlier, Antoine Furetière had the opposite notion – for him a title was akin to a good book's hustler. When I first proposed *Oublier Camus* (*Forget Camus*) to my French publisher, they hesitated, worried the title might be too provocative: it would offend booksellers, alarm readers, hurt sales. I was more concerned it would simply be ignored – as many predecessors had been. Yves Ancel wrote a superb monograph in 2012, and though it remains in print, it is, as far as reviews are concerned, largely exiled. Exile was quite literally the case for Christiane Chaulet-Achour's latest and excellent book: it could only find a publisher in Italy. Going further back in time, Edward Said's masterpiece *Culture and Imperialism*, which included a brilliant chapter on Camus, was published in France seven long years after it appeared in the United States, having been willfully ignored by major French publishers.

The mainstream press's reaction to my book was anger – outrage, even – which was actually something of a relief. The reviews formed a numerous and unlikely coalition. Call it a national front of the Camusians: professors, novelists, critics, former ministers, editorialists, all claiming to be the true heirs of the same man. It began with an anarchist weekly urging

---

1   Translation: 'One does not abdicate the honour of being a target.'

readers to forget Gloag rather than Camus – a verdict echoed, from the other wing of the French political theater, by the cultural critic for the hard-right daily *Le Figaro*, who confessed to almost choking with rage upon reading *Oublier Camus*. Around the same time came pieces in *L'Express*, *Le Point*, *Marianne*, *Le Monde*, *Slate* – one contributor boasting that he had not read the book and disliked it all the same – a trail reaching to the far-right online publication *Causeur*. All of this led a renowned scholar to ask, with deliberate irony, what exactly Oliver Gloag's crime had been. There were several.

The first was blasphemy: daring to criticize a sacred figure. In French cultural life, Camus is what one of his former mentors called him: a secular saint. Today, one might say that he has also become a humanist commodity icon, precious to France's official self-image. In France, literature is everything; as Sartre observed, the literature of an age is that age digested by its literature. To dare to touch Camus is to touch something the French state in its current form needs to preserve – pure, intact, untouched.

The second offense had to do with France's bitter obsession with Algeria. To write about France's 132-year occupation – its concentration camps, organized massacres, apartheid-like legislation, systematic dispossession – and to document Camus's double standard for victims (one measure of compassion for the settlers, another for the colonized fighting for their freedom) was to draw a line the French intelligentsia prefers to leave undrawn: from colonial past to neocolonial present, from Algeria to New Caledonia, to Palestine.

This obsession with Algeria can be explained in part because France is a country haunted by its defeats. This is by design. The target of national resentment shifts with the epoch – the English (Agincourt, Waterloo), the Germans (Battle of Sedan, the Occupation), now the Algerians – performing, as Charles de Gaulle theorized, the domestic function of displacing class from the center of French political life.

The third offense was an alleged attack on Camus himself. This is simply not the case. This book is an attempt to contextualize him – historically, politically, literarily – and to examine a canonization (and the canonizers themselves, those who have furthered their own careers by praising Camus endlessly) that has reached, in France, something close to paroxysm. Yet to contextualize him also means acknowledging what was admirable about him. Camus was among the few public voices in France to write against the atomic bombings of Hiroshima and Nagasaki. That Camus, shaped in part by the Popular Front, is also in this book. The challenge here is to read Camus without, as the author and scholar Vincent Berthelier put it, lying to oneself.

Not everyone was outraged. Outside the *doxa*, or conventional wisdom, other voices responded differently. The novelist and critic Arnaud Viviant called my book '*l'essai de l'année*' (essay of the year). The non-colonial left was largely sympathetic, as were, notably, many Algerian novelists, scholars, journalists, and readers.

At book talks, students have often told me of their exasperation at being taught *The Stranger* as a fable in which the killing of an Algerian man on a beach is a mere pretext for discussing ostensibly more weighty philosophical issues. Their frustration is, in many ways, this book's starting point.

A word, finally, about why *Oublier Camus* was written in French. To fully grasp the intensity of France's bond with the author of *The Stranger*, one has to be steeped in French culture, in its literature, and sensitive to the particular charge the name 'Camus' carries – in any French conversation, political debate, or argument about national identity. But to see that bond clearly – to examine it rather than simply feel it – one also has to be, in some measure, an outsider. I am both.

Which brings us back to the title. To forget Camus is not to dismiss him – it is a provocative paradox and a challenge not to idolize him but, on the contrary, to take him seriously.

One has to know Camus well, and know his times, in order to forget the airbrushed figure presented to us, again and again, by the guardians of culture.

Oliver Gloag
New York City, March 2026

Preface

Fredric Jameson

Universalism is no happy accident of nature; it is generality wrenched free from the particulars of a concrete situation, a concrete experience. Most often, it is mediated by a common language or, as in the case of Europe, by a common system of languages. It is therefore most dramatic, most visible, in coloniality and in the illusion of universality perpetuated by the language of the colonizer, as James Joyce observed for Irish literature in its greatest period. One is also tempted to suggest something similar for the generation of Franco Algerians that followed Camus (Derrida, Cixous, Attali, Althusser, and so on) – a rich intellectual moment indeed. But when, with the war, Camus moved to the mainland, something different, something more problematic, began to take place.

This is why it is important to grasp his first works, what Alice Kaplan has called his trilogy, as prewar achievements, despite their wartime publication dates. Novel, play, philosophical text, it has a horizontal coherence (death, *le bonheur*) along with a vertical or linguistic one; and these two intersecting dimensions make for an unrepeatable and unique linguistic experiment. That of *The Stranger* and its wholly uncolloquial narrative in the *passé composé* is known to the general reader; but *Caligula*'s unspeakable language lessons in death, the impossible philosophizing of *The Myth of Sisyphus* about happiness – these two parts of *The Stranger* that do not add up – these remain to be appreciated for the extraordinary feat of language production they represent, and which Camus would never again achieve. In France, they were replaced by a linguistic *mauvaise foi* which Oliver Gloag's book goes a long way towards situating, if not explaining; the sharing of the language of the metropole, indeed, suddenly, began to trouble the brilliant blue sky of a colonial language, a linguistic Tipasa. In Algeria, Camus could be critical and as anti-colonial as he would ever be; in France, things were more complicated, and the revolution asked him to take sides, which he was unwilling and perhaps unable to do.

The critique of Camus also asks us, unfairly, to take sides; and it is convenient to have Sartre to take sides against (or, as here perhaps, for). But how can we appreciate Camus's positions and the literary production they involve without some rudimentary knowledge of his situation? Any more than we can appreciate the meaning of his dramatization of a *bonheur* outside of time without equally feeling the horror and immediacy of his premonitions of death?

As you read this book, it will become apparent that its critique is aimed not so much at Camus himself as at his middle-brow canonization; and at the canonization of his image rather than his work, at that. With this, we enter a political debate rather than a literary one, a debate which features the appropriation of art for ideological purposes, and which demands analysis in its own right (even though the writer may well be complicit in the process).

Politically minded Camus enthusiasts, indeed, may well be surprised by how poorly their image of him corresponds to the works themselves. To be sure, the anti-communism they want to associate him with becomes ever more pronounced until his untimely death. But it has little enough to do with the early trilogy, in which Caligula sets out to demonstrate the value of life by his lethal pedagogy. But readers of this book – on the left as well as the right – will be astonished to find the roots of this seemingly Mediterranean vitalism in the Popular Front and the optimistic political energies of that period, a background more durable than the alleged heroism of a Resistance which was, in any case, a peculiarly French configuration, essentially anti-fascist and pro-Soviet in character. Unsurprisingly, the postwar era brought political complications with it which forced French intellectuals into painful choices between the US and the Soviet Union. In the case of Camus, these choices were overlaid by specifically Algerian choices between colonialism and liberation which made for the contradictions he was unable to master in his later works. These are contradictions which could often be masked as purely ethical choices between violence and sacrifice, when they were not altogether evacuated as purely philosophical questions.

The present book develops the background against which Camus's literary and ideological strategies – agonizing as they may have been – alone become intelligible. They make it impossible to use him as some vaguely liberal and humanist icon, thereby freeing him from manipulation by the political establishment and allowing us to measure the true and complex originality of a historic work endangered by an apolitical propaganda in the service of even more unacceptable anti-political seductions.

Introduction

I have to confess (just between us) that I'm a bit confused. Yes, Camus was religious, but without faith; a moralist, but without philosophy; a writer, but without style. So what then? How did all these deficiencies produce a celebrated man of letters?
   – Jean Paulhan, letter to Jean Guéhenno, January 1960[1]

What do George W. Bush, an African American sentenced to death in Indiana, the French far right, the Anarchist Federation, *Le Figaro*, *L'Humanité*, Hollywood stars, and several Arab anti-colonial intellectuals have in common?

All of them lay claim to Camus's legacy.

Camus is everywhere: in movies, in television series (Netflix, Amazon), in journals and magazines, on the stage, in newspapers, on T-shirts – and in books. He is solemnly invoked by all kinds of people, always in a reverent tone. Sometimes, Camus is embraced sincerely – like a believer calling upon a saint – but, far more often, he is co-opted in a more cynical fashion.

Take the case of Emmanuel Macron. Shortly before his election in 2017, he repeatedly professed to the media his admiration for Camus's work, especially the lyrical *Nuptials at Tipasa*.[2] Yet this text finds its source in everything Macron is bent on dismantling, namely the social conquests of the

---

1   Jean Paulhan, *Choix de lettres vol. III*, Paris: Gallimard, 1996, 162. My translation.
2   Franz-Olivier Giesbert, 'Le fils du soleil et du vent', *Le Figaro*, 19 April 2017; Vincent Tremolet de Villers, 'Macron, le choix des mots pour effacer des faits', *Le Figaro*, 17 April 2017.

labour movement – those hard-won rights are the very condition of its possibility. The context is as follows. The strikes and factory occupations of May–June 1936 transformed the lives of many people in metropolitan France; the Matignon Agreements, beyond wage increases, inaugurated a new way of life, thanks to reduced working hours (from forty-eight to forty hours per week), but, above all, to the first paid holidays: two weeks. Everything changed. The French discovered the countryside, cycling, the beach, the mountains. In *Nuptials at Tipasa*,[3] which he began in 1937, the young *pied-noir* office clerk Albert Camus developed his theory of *bonheur*: fleeting moments of intense communion with nature. Camusian happiness expresses this new reality born of a profound social upheaval.

His attachment to social emancipation, however, was subordinated to other interests. In an article from October 1938, 'Speculation against Social Laws',[4] Camus – then a journalist and editorial writer at *Alger républicain* – expressed concern for the gains of the strikes of May–June 1936. He rightly protested against the fact that wage increases were nullified by rising prices and proposed that they be indexed to the cost of living. Camus also pointed to the disparity between the wage increases of those he called 'indigenous labourers (non-Moroccan)' (whom we will call Algerians) and 'European workers' (whom we will call *pieds-noirs*).[5] Camus noted that the wages of pieds-noirs had increased by 20 percent, whereas those of Algerians had increased by 60 percent. Let us note

---

3   Albert Camus, 'Nuptials at Tipasa', in *Lyrical and Critical Essays*, New York: Vintage Books, 1982, 65–73.

4   Albert Camus, 'La speculation contre les lois sociales', in *Œuvres complètes*, vol. I, Paris: Gallimard, 2006, 575–6. My translation.

5   At the beginning of the twentieth century, the term *pieds-noirs* (lit. 'black feet') referred to Algerian sailors who worked barefoot on coal transport ships. During the Algerian War of Independence, its meaning shifted to designate people of French and other European descent born in Algeria during the period of French colonial rule from 1830 to 1962.

what did not shock Camus: the actual hourly wages of each group – Algerians earning, after the strikes, 2.30 francs an hour and pieds-noirs 7.20 francs. Camus did not question this glaring injustice; on the contrary, he treated it as an absolute given in his calculations – an acceptance of the imperial axiom that Europeans earn more than Algerians for equal work. What shocked Camus was that pied-noir workers had not received a 60 percent increase like the Algerians. He sought to maintain the inequality between the colonized and colonizers and took offence when it was not respected. Camus defended both the gains of the strikes of 1936 *and* the colonial order. Camus is fundamentally divided: he brings new realities into view while, at the same time, ratifying older ones, which he normalizes and which form the backdrop of his work.

Invoking Camus has become a way of asserting a humanism that is as vague as it is ostentatious.

The literary, political, and cultural fields, in a rare display of unanimity, set about fashioning Camus into a secular saint:[6] a humanist, a philosopher, an anti-colonial activist, an early member of the Resistance, a man devoted to justice and opposed to the death penalty, and a great writer. This vision – in the literal sense of the word – accords with a France engaged in the repression of its imperial past and the denial of its neocolonial present.

---

6 The expression comes from Pascal Pia, who stated after his mentee received the Nobel Prize: 'Camus resembles less a rebel than a secular saint': Albert Camus, *Œuvres complètes,* vol. IV, Paris: Gallimard, 2008, 274. My translation.

1

For a Colonialism with a Human Face

The rise of Algerian nationalism emerges from the persecutions to which it is subjected. It will no longer have any reason to exist when injustice disappears from this country.
> – Albert Camus, 'The Progress of Algerian
> Nationalism, Letter from Algiers'[1]

One cannot approach Camus without evoking the history of the country he believed to be his own. It is essential to resituate Camus's positions on colonialism within their historical context, which requires – if only briefly – an examination of the French presence in Algeria. That presence began in 1830, but systematic colonization begins in earnest only in 1870 with the return of the Republic.[2]

Let us note that we will refer to the Arab-Berber peoples who lived in Algeria before and during the French occupation as 'Algerians' or 'the Algerian people', rather than using the colonial terms 'natives' or 'Muslims'. We will refer to the colonists as pieds-noirs or 'European Algerians', depending on context. As one of the preeminent historians of the period, Charles-Robert Ageron, explains, 'The Europeans of Algeria aggressively declared themselves "Algerians" whenever they encountered difficulties with the Metropole, and, conversely, asserted themselves as "French" when conflicts arose with the

---

1   Albert Camus, *Méditerranée-Afrique du Nord*, June 1939, in *Œuvres complètes*, vol. I, Paris: Gallimard, 2006, 873. My translation.

2   Abd el-Kader's military campaigns and resistance activity will be more closely examined in Chapter 2.

Muslims.'[3] Referring to colonists as 'Algerians' would therefore amount to a form of dispossession. Even today, some commentators still describe Camus as an 'Algerian writer'; such language betrays a nostalgia for a time when colonization was taken for granted.[4]

Colony and Metropole: Diverging Paths

Under the Second Empire (1852–70), Algeria was effectively under French military control. In 1860, the emperor and his army publicly recognized the principle of Arab sovereignty. In February 1863, Napoleon III wrote: 'Algeria is not, properly speaking, a colony, but an Arab kingdom.'[5] During a visit to Algeria in 1865, he added:

> France has not come to destroy the nationality of a people ... I wish to improve your well-being, to enable you to participate ever more fully in the administration of your country, as well as in the benefits of civilization.[6]

He had a decree issued stipulating that the Algerian was the equal of Frenchman, that he could apply for naturalization and thereby gain access to full civic rights.[7] The French settlers in Algeria launched a campaign against the 'Emperor

---

3 Charles-Robert Ageron, *Histoire de L'Algérie contemporaine (1830–1994)*, Paris: Presses Universitaires de France, 1994, 85. My translation.

4 On the contrary, when Kamel Daoud describes Camus as an 'Algerian writer', it is not an expression of colonial nostalgia, but of a change in the balance of power: the newly independent nation is now the inviting power.

5 Ageron, *Histoire de L'Algérie contemporaine*, 30–1.

6 Ibid., 31.

7 The on-the-ground reality was wholly different: a whole judicial apparatus enabled the expropriation of Algerian land by the occupying forces.

of the Arabs',[8] and, from that point onward, throughout the final ninety-two years of French rule, two major tendencies would clash. On the one hand, the metropole favoured indirect control with some degree of Algerian participation – a position embodied over time by Napoleon III, Clemenceau, Viollette, and, ultimately, Camus himself. On the other hand, the majority of French settlers in Algeria, backed by a powerful parliamentary lobby, sought – and obtained – absolute domination and control of the Algerian population.[9]

In 1870, the fall of the Second Empire and the advent of the Third Republic amounted, in concrete terms, to a victory for the settlers. They gradually took control of nearly the entire territory and reduced Algerians to the status of French subjects governed by a separate set of laws. In 1881, the *Code de l'indigénat* legally defined the status of Algerians, rendering them effectively subhumans: they could neither vote nor travel without official permission; they were subject to special tribunals (and liable to imprisonment for the slightest infraction) and burdened with punitive taxation. Deprived of all rights, Algerians were, nonetheless, subject to all the obligations of French citizens, including compulsory military service.

This citizenship, denied to Muslims, was imposed on Algerian Jews, whom France designated as 'Indigenous Israelites'. In 1865, when the metropole decided to attempt to dilute settler power and win over a segment of the indigenous population to the colonial cause – a classic imperial strategy – Algerian Jews were offered naturalization on a voluntary, individual basis. Almost none accepted, and for good reason: they had no greater connection to France than the other peoples of Algeria. Culturally and linguistically, they were Arab. Faced with this near-unanimous refusal, the French state responded

---

8   Ageron, *Histoire de L'Algérie contemporaine*, 32.

9   These two apparently opposed positions ultimately converge. They differ only in method, for both rest on the principle of a legitimacy derived from conquest by force.

by unilaterally naturalizing all Algerian Jews in 1870. They became French citizens by way of legal coercion.[10]

The European settlers saw this decision as an affront to their privileges and, worse still, as a potential harbinger of future naturalizations. From that point on, a torrent of hostility was unleashed against these new French citizens. The virulent anti-semitism of the European settlers created an atmosphere of constant denigration and gave rise to frequent and unpunished lethal violence – from pogroms in Oran (1897) and Constan-tine (1934), to the creation of a highly popular 'anti-Jewish party', and the publication of mass-circulation newspapers bearing the swastika on their front pages in the 1930s.[11] Anti-semitism and anti-Muslim racism were the hallmark of French Algeria until its disappearance in 1962.

It was only in 1918, in the aftermath of the First World War, that the metropole once again seriously attempted to intervene directly and over the long term in the functioning of the colony. After the exorbitant sacrifices made by the Algerian people during the conflict – nearly one third of Algerian men took part in the war effort – and in light of the growing political influence of Algerian elites[12] organized into pressure groups (such as the Jeunes Algériens), who sought political equality with the French within an assimilationist framework, Georges Clemenceau, during his second term as head of government (1917–20), proposed political compensations for the colonized

---

10 'By resorting to legal coercion, Justice Minister Adolphe Crémieux, who had spent his life fighting against abuses of power, ultimately embraced, for the sake of expediency, the logic of *compelle intrare*': Charles-André Julien, *Histoire de l'Algérie contemporaine (1827–1871)*, vol. I, Paris: Presses Universitaires de France, 1964, 467. My translation.

11 Ageron, *Histoire de l'Algérie contemporaine*, vol. II, 367–8.

12 Members of the Algerian elite – that is, bourgeois Algerians edu-cated within the French system – were referred to, in characteristically paternalistic fashion, as *évolués* ('evolved') by both European settlers and most metropolitan French.

population. These proposals included allowing Algerian elected representatives to participate alongside settlers in legislative and senatorial elections. In matters of taxation, Algerians would have been subject to the same rates as settlers. Charles Jonnart, the short-lived governor of Algeria (1918–19) and a close associate of Clemenceau, also sought to relax the *Code de l'indigénat* by abolishing special courts. This project weakened Jonnart – derisively nicknamed 'Jonnart the Muslim' by pied-noir notables, their parliamentary representatives, and their allies in the Parisian press. Under pressure, he remained in office for only one year. Neither Jonnart's bill nor Clemenceau's proposals came to fruition.

The sequence was repeated a few years later under the governorship of Maurice Viollette (1925–7), sent from the metropole and quickly convinced of the need to reform colonial legislation in Algeria. What motivated this conviction was fear of contagion. Viollette governed during the Rif War in Morocco (1921–6), in which Spain first, and then France, suffered a long series of defeats at the hands of the popular army led by Abd el-Krim. These events made metropolitan elites acutely aware of the urgency of adopting a more conciliatory stance towards the Algerian population in order to avoid a similar armed uprising. As governor-general, Viollette publicly stated that el-Krim had to be removed from the political scene at all costs, which confirms his ultimate objective: to prevent the emergence of Algerian independence.[13] For this reason, Viollette became a sworn enemy of the Communists in Algeria, who supported the Rif leader's struggle through their press organs (*La Lutte sociale*, *Le Paria*, and *L'Humanité*).

It was in the spirit of a short-term, objective alliance in the face of the danger of armed insurrection that French settlers temporarily tolerated Viollette despite his proposals, which included, among other measures, voluntary access to French

---

13   Ageron, *Histoire de l'Algérie contemporaine*, vol. II, 299.

citizenship for all Algerians. Faced with these concessions, Algerian elites were divided. In light of pied-noir hostility and the Jonnart precedent, some leaders abandoned their assimilationist demands and began calling for a degree of autonomy; these were led by one of the grandsons of Emir Abd el-Kader, whom the colonial authorities had convicted, and who spent the remainder of his life in exile in Damascus.

Once Abd el-Krim had been neutralized, the alliance between the pieds-noirs and the French metropolitan elite no longer had any raison d'être. Shortly after Viollette's November 1927 proposal to 'grant the indigenous elite the right to vote alongside the French', the pied-noir deputies Gaston Thomson and Émile Morinaud obtained the immediate recall of 'Viollette the Arab', on 9 November 1927.[14]

Viollette did not concede defeat. Three years after his removal from the governorship, he renewed his effort and, in July 1931, introduced the bill that bears his name. The Viollette proposal (later renamed 'Blum–Viollette') abolished the *Code de l'indigénat* and granted French citizenship (and therefore the right to vote) to a minority of Algerian men – 21,000 out of 900,000, or less than 3 percent.

Camus Supports Viollette

At the age of twenty-three, in April 1937, Albert Camus fervently supported the 'Blum–Viollette' project. According to the editors of his *Œuvres complètes*, he was a coauthor of a manifesto in support of the proposal, in which one can discern a line of reasoning – granting more rights to Algerian elites would bring them over to France's side: 'Considering that, far from harming the interests of France, this project serves them in the most immediate way, insofar as it will present to the

---

14 Ageron, *Modern Algeria*, 74.

Arab people the face of humanity that France must embody.'[15] Yet, in 1937, Algerian elites were even less convinced than they had been in the 1920s of the willingness of the pieds-noirs to share power, and, above all, of the capacity of the metropole to impose even this modest reform on the settlers. The many initiatives and approaches of the Jeunes Algériens ended in refusals. Other Algerian organizations, notably the North African Star, which had come under the control of Messali Hadj, rejected the Blum–Viollette project outright, judging that it was designed to separate the masses from the elites and would have created a pro-colonial indigenous elite in Algeria (they were punished for their lucidity: Hadj was thrown into prison). Even when reformist *ulama* gathered around the weekly *Chihâb* supported the idea, they did so only because the bill was seen as a step towards independence.

Faced with the rise of nationalism among Algerian elites who had largely abandoned their assimilationist hopes, two opposing strategies emerged. The vast majority of settlers categorically rejected any concession whatsoever. A small minority, by contrast – generally from the left, close to the Communist Party and the Socialists (Section Française de l'Internationale Ouvrière, or SFIO) – believed that granting certain rights to a small Algerian elite was the best way to neutralize any drive towards independence. A fundamental divide therefore split colonial circles. Advocates of compromise – intended to save the empire – warned the hardliners that their stance risked pushing Algerians towards independence. As early as 1931, Viollette issued this prophetic warning:

> In fifteen or twenty years, there will be more than ten million natives in Algeria, among whom nearly one million men and women imbued with French culture. Are we going to turn them

---

15 Camus, 'Manifeste des intellectuels d'Algérie en faveur du projet Viollette', in *Œuvres complètes*, vol. I, 573. My translation.

into rebels, or French citizens? Will we be so blinded by what some consider their immediate material interest to sacrifice our African empire and the fate of the country? ... If that were the case, and if the metropole did not intervene to impose a more just and more humane point of view, [French] Algeria would be doomed.[16]

Camus would make this analysis his own – formulating it in different ways – throughout his life. This line of argument draws its strength (and its weakness) from its ambiguity: is he defending the rights of the 'Arab people' in order to achieve full equality, as he sometimes suggests? Or is his aim to limit the anger and unity of the Algerian people so as not to call the colonial power structure into question?

The first interpretation is so often repeated that it has taken on the status of dogma in France. One thing is certain: Camus plays on this ambiguity. His disciple and friend, the pied-noir poet Jean Sénac, called him his 'serpentine brother', in reference to the studied ambiguity of his positions.[17]

In any case, this modest attempt to reform the colonial system ended in yet another failure. The Blum–Viollette bill provoked a threat of collective resignation by almost all the mayors of French Algeria and was never even debated in the national assembly. After this defeat, the Communist Party in Algeria completely changed its strategy, moving towards support for independence, a path that would lead, nearly twenty years later, to its merger with the Front de Libération Nationale (FLN). As Ageron notes:

After the definitive failure of the Blum–Viollette project, the Communist Party once again insisted on the Arab-Muslim character of Algeria and on the necessity of education in Arabic,

---

16 Ageron, *Modern Algeria*, 74.

17 Hamid Nacer-Khodja, *Albert Camus, Jean Sénac ou le fils rebelle*, Paris: Éditions Paris-Méditerranée, 2004, 56. My translation.

while a slight majority was granted to Algerian members within the political bureau.[18]

It was at this point, in 1937, that Camus left the Algerian Communist Party and withdrew for a time from political activity. Henri Alleg – former director of *Alger républicain*, former member of the Algerian Communist Party, author of *The Question*, the famous book on torture during the War of Independence, and a historic figure in the struggle for independence – clarifies the situation:

> Contrary to what he may have suggested, Albert Camus did not leave the Algerian Communist Party because he favoured a 'national' Algeria while the Communists were opposed to it. He left the Algerian Communist Party at the very moment when it began to defend national positions![19]

Only two years later, as a journalist, did Camus once again attempt to influence pied-noir public opinion. In a series of articles based on his reporting in Kabylia, published in June 1939, one finds the same strategy as Viollette's: humanitarianism in the service of colonialism.

In 'Misery in Kabylia',[20] Camus recounts his encounter with young Kabyle children who ask him for food; he describes their outstretched hands as 'emaciated'.[21] He is shown a child who is 'frail and ragged'; her grandfather asks him, 'If I could

---

18   Ageron, *Histoire de l'Algérie contemporaine*, vol. II, 385. My translation.

19   Lamria Chetouani, 'Entretien avec Henri Alleg', *Mots: Les langages du politique*, no. 57 (1998): 109–29, at 125. My translation.

20   Camus would go on to republish these articles twenty years later as a collection entitled *The Misery of Kabylia* (1958). Releasing it in the midst of the Algerian War of Independence as proof of his reformist commitments, he omitted several pieces with an explicitly paternalistic tone, including 'Greece in Rags'. Camus, *Œuvres complètes*, vol. I, 653–6 (first published as 'La Grèce en haillons' in *Alger républicain*, 5 June 1939). My translation.

21   Ibid., 654.

keep her clean and feed her, wouldn't she be as beautiful as any French girl?' At the sight of her, Camus exclaims: 'I felt a guilty conscience – one that I should not have been the only one to feel.'[22] This desire to extract a Kabyle girl from her abject poverty so that she might be like 'any French girl' reveals the ambition behind this charity: inclusion within the colonial order, belonging to the family of France.

Camus also explains to his readers that it is in the colony's interests to be 'generous', meaning not to let Kabyles starve. Throughout these articles – addressed primarily to pied-noir readers – he shares his guilty conscience while describing in great detail the sordid living conditions in Kabylia, but without explaining that the French state's neglect was deliberate and repressive, since, historically, the Kabyles had mounted some of the most determined resistance to the occupier. The staging of a humanitarian drama does not lead to questioning the legitimacy of the colonial order. It allows the author to express colonial discomfort without having to condemn the institutions responsible for this state of affairs.

He had hoped that his articles on Kabylia in *Alger républicain* would spark a moment of reckoning among the pieds-noirs and the governing authorities. The opposite occurred. The daily newspaper directed by Pascal Pia and Albert Camus was ultimately banned by the colonial authorities in October 1939, in part because of these articles and also because of its pacifist positions.

His inability to influence colonial circles plunged Camus into a profound disillusionment, all the more so because it coincided with other setbacks. Personal: his marriage to his first wife began to fracture when, during a trip to Europe, he learned that she was cheating on him.[23] Professional: his long

---

22 Ibid.

23 This, according to Patrick McCarthy, would become the source of his Don Juanism: *Camus: A Critical Study of His Life and Work*, London: Hamish Hamilton, 1982, 80.

university studies came to nothing; upon completing them, he was barred from teaching by the French state on account of tuberculosis. From these disappointments emerged both a detachment that was as absolute as it was ostentatious, and the idea that the world makes no sense, that it is devoid of logic and morality – an absurd world.[24]

The absurd in Camus paradoxically constitutes a system and a way of giving meaning to a world that has none. According to Camus, there are two forms of the absurd. The first states a fact: neither life nor death has meaning. The second issues an injunction: one must live one's life as an 'absurd man', accepting that human intelligence is incapable of providing meaning to the world. Camus consequently takes refuge in the rejection of knowledge, of the Enlightenment, of History; in this way he turns his back on the problems – insoluble in his view – posed by colonialism. He then cultivates an aesthetic relationship with Algeria. He returns to politics only when compelled by the events of the Second World War.

In January 1944, in Brazzaville – and earlier in Algiers and Constantine – General de Gaulle suggested that the independence of colonized peoples would be granted as a reward for their commitment alongside France against Nazi Germany:

> There would be no progress that could truly be called progress ... if they could not, at home, take part in the management of their own affairs. It is the duty of France to ensure that this is the case.[25]

---

24   This sense of detachment is striking in *The Stranger*, with Meursault having mysteriously abandoned both his studies and his ambitions.

25   Charles de Gaulle, 'Discours prononcé par le général de Gaulle', in *La Conférence africaine française: Brazaville 30 janvier – 8 février 1944*, Brazaville: éditions du Baobab, 1944.

The Army of Africa, particularly the Algerian riflemen, composed of 80 percent Algerians (referred to as *Indigènes*),[26] contributed directly to France's first military victories in Europe during the Italian campaign.

This dishonest Gaullist promise, France's retreat, the loss of its military prestige, and the living conditions of the colonized populations sparked challenges to colonial authority throughout the French Empire in the immediate postwar period, notably in Senegal, Cameroon, and Syria.[27] All were drowned in blood. In a large number of colonies, demonstrations for independence were widely supported by veterans returning from the European front. They had fulfilled their part of the bargain.

The Algerian People's Party (PPA) called for demonstrations on 8 May 1945 in Sétif and Guelma, demanding the release of its leader, Messali Hadj – imprisoned by the French authorities since April 1944 – as well as Algerian independence. These demonstrations in northern Constantinois[28] turned into riots in Sétif following police intervention, as the authorities attempted to prevent demonstrators by force from raising the Algerian flag or expressing nationalist demands in any form. Pied-noir civilians were killed. The entire region rose up, and the French army then waged a genuine war against Algerian civilians until 24 May. The air force dropped forty-one tons of bombs on insurgent villages; the French navy also carried out

---

26 The eponymous film directed by Rachid Bouchareb – *Days of Glory* (2006) in English – recalls that the veterans of these units were stripped of their military pensions by the French state after Algeria gained independence. Rachid Bouchareb (dir.), *Indigènes* (*Days of Glory*), France/Algeria/Morocco/Belgium: Tessalit Productions/Kissfilms Productions et al., 2006.

27 Yves Benot, *Massacres coloniaux* (Colonial massacres), Paris: La Découverte, 2001; and the long-censored film by Ousmane Sembène, *Camp de Thiaroye* (1988).

28 Jean-Pierre Peyroulou, 'Les massacres du Nord-Constantinois de 1945, un événement polymorphe', in *Histoire de l'Algérie à la période coloniale, 1830–1962*, ed. Abderrahmane Bouchène et al., Paris: La Découverte, 2012, 502–8.

bombardments, while the army fired 858 artillery shells. Pied-noir militias joined the French army. The death toll is debated, but the dead number in the thousands: 10,000 according to a French intelligence officer, 17,000 according to the US army. These figures show that this was not a simple repression but a state-sanctioned massacre of civilian populations. No settler was punished, no officer of the French army was held accountable; the army executed hundreds of Algerian civilians after sham trials.

Camus was reporting in Algeria when these bloodbaths took place. Upon his return to Paris, he published a series of articles. One of them evokes a fever of 'disordered desires for power and expansion' that 'will never be excused unless we compensate for them with an attentive will toward justice and unwavering dedication'.[29] He is speaking here obliquely about Sétif and Guelma. In the end, he devoted only a few lines to them – brief, but revealing: 'The massacres of Guelma and Sétif provoked among the French of Algeria a deep and indignant resentment. The repression that followed fostered among the Arab masses a sense of fear and hostility.'[30] For Camus, the 'massacres' therefore refer to the hundred or so pied-noir deaths. By contrast, the killing of more than 10,000 Algerian civilians – systematically murdered by the army, the police, and pied-noir militias – is designated by the discreet term 'repression'.

What emerges from these lines is clear: when Europeans kill Algerians by the thousands, it is described as force; when the reverse occurs, and on a far smaller scale, it is described as violence.[31] It should also be noted that Camus says nothing about

---

29 Albert Camus, 'C'est la justice qui sauvera l'Algérie de la haine', *Combat*, 23 May 1945, in *Camus à Combat*, Paris: Gallimard, 2002, 530.

30 Albert Camus, 'Crise en Algérie', *Combat*, 21 May 1945, in *Œuvres complètes*, vol. IV, 2008, 351.

31 This is Max Weber's concept of the monopoly on violence as

the living conditions of Algerians during the Second World War – which were materially far harsher than those of the pieds-noirs or metropolitan French – nothing about aspirations to independence. Camus sanctions the presence and authority of the French state in Algeria through carefully chosen words and notable omissions. Some human beings are more equal than others: only some have the right to revolt.

According to Camus, even after the massacres of Sétif, Guelma, and Kherrata, France must remain an 'Arab power'.[32] This, in his view, is the only way for France to preserve its status as a colonial power and continue to be 'treated with consideration'. He then explains to his readers that France must undertake a second conquest[33] of the Algerian people: it must convince them of the legitimacy of colonialism. Camus calls for the invention of 'new formulas' and the need to 'rejuvenate our methods', conceding that this conquest 'will be less easy than the first'.[34] He also proposes concrete measures. His 23 May 1945 article in *Combat*, entitled 'Justice Will Save Algeria from Hatred', includes a call to intensify colonization:

> We therefore need new men. And at a time when so many young French people are searching for a path and a reason to live, we may perhaps find a few thousand among them who will understand that a land awaits them, where they will be able to serve both humanity and their country.[35]

Camus does not speak of settlers but of 'the anxious conquerors we are', and insists that they must learn from the 'wisdom offered by Arab civilization'.[36] These awkward oxymorons and

---

applied to the colonial state: when the state exercises it, it is legitimate; when the colonized resists, it is illegitimate.

32 Camus, 'Interview in *Servir*', in *Œuvres complètes*, vol. II, 660.

33 Camus, 'Crise en Algérie', 339.

34 Camus had just returned to Algeria in May 1945, when he published a series of articles from 12 to 25 May.

35 Camus, 'C'est la justice qui sauvera l'Algérie de la haine', 530.

36 Ibid.

declamatory formulations, which irritated many at the time, are likely signs of his growing disarray in the face of the rising strength of the independence movement.

What is certain is that this second conquest failed before it even began.

A year and a half later, Camus published a series of articles entitled 'Neither Victims nor Executioners',[37] in which he appears to place the colonized and colonizers on the same footing, at a time when anti-colonialism was gaining momentum worldwide. This would be the final expression of Camus's proclaimed neutrality.

In private, however, his reaction after the French defeat in Indochina at Dien Bien Phu reveals where his sympathies lay. The day after the defeat, on 8 May 1954, he compared, in his notebook, the Indochinese liberating their country to the Germans invading France:

> Fall of Dien Bien Phu. As in '40, a mixture of shame and fury. On the evening of the massacre, the reckoning is clear. Right-wing politicians placed unfortunate men in an indefensible position, while at the same time men of the Left were shooting them in the back.[38]

This double game between his public statements and his private opinions led to a break with his friend and former disciple, the poet Jean Sénac. A pied-noir from a poor background, like Camus himself, Sénac had moved closer to the independence movement. He gradually lost patience with his mentor's evasions. In his correspondence – a letter to Camus dated December 1957 – he tells him bluntly:

> I constantly note this tragic oscillation, these contradictions, this misunderstanding, this equivocation in the use of words,

---

37 Camus, 'Ni Victimes ni bourreaux', in *Œuvres complètes*, vol. II, 436–56.

38 Camus, *Carnets 1949–1959*, in *Œuvres complètes*, vol. IV, 1184.

which belong at once to an honest man and to an unacceptable hypocrite[39] playing on registers too imprecise for the melody to emerge.[40]

Sénac also denounced Camus publicly, in a manifesto of poetic struggle: 'The one who writes will never be equal to those who die, Camus once declared, at a time when he had not yet repudiated the injustice of *The Just Assassins*.'[41] It was the day after the publication of this critique that Camus decided to fall silent 'with regard to Algeria'.[42]

Pressed by events, he became the voice of yet another compromise: a detailed project for sharing power between pieds-noirs and Algerians, in which France would retain all sovereign prerogatives – justice, the economy, and the army. This project closely resembles what former French colonies in Africa later became, under the system known as 'Françafrique'. In the end, he openly expressed support for the 'dubious theses'[43] of Marc Lauriol, an ultra pied-noir. In the same article, he described the project of Algerian independence as a 'purely emotional slogan'.[44]

A Useful Icon

Camus never managed to resolve the contradiction between republican humanism and colonialism. Yet, today, he is

---

39   *Louette* in the French, which means clever, sly, or cunning in Algerian pied-noir slang.

40   Cited by Nacer-Khodja in *Albert Camus, Jean Sénac ou le fils rebelle*, 95. My translation.

41   Ibid., 87. My translation.

42   Albert Camus, *Essais*, Paris: Gallimard, 1965, 1843.

43   The expression is from Albert-Paul Lentin, cited in Pierre Nora, *Les Français d'Algérie*, Paris: Christian Bourgois, 2012, 308. My translation.

44   Camus, 'Algérie 1958', in *Œuvres complètes*, 388. My translation.

consecrated as the emblem of an impossible synthesis. Camus is a useful icon; he embodies an incantatory solution.

In reality, Camus was in no sense an anti-colonialist, but, rather, a subtle defender of a humanist compromise aimed at preserving the French presence in Algeria. He had understood that the intransigence of the pieds-noirs risked accelerating independence; his ambition never went beyond a reform of the colonial system. Why, then, present Camus as an anti-colonialist? Because through the romanticized image of a Camus who is simultaneously a settler and anti-colonialist, one can promote the image of a France that is colonial yet equally devoted to justice. Through the idealization of Camus, it is the history of France itself that is mythologized.

Of these two causes – humanism and French Algeria – Camus did in fact choose the latter. The mask fell when he told Roger Quilliot, in September 1959, 'If Algeria becomes independent, I will leave France. I will go to Canada.'[45]

One can trace the stages of his slow and painful trajectory – rendered almost invisible by its reception in France – which runs from denial to repression, and finally to the emergence of the colonial question, across his three major works: *The Stranger*, *The Plague*, and *The First Man*.

---

45 Camus, *Essais*, 1861.

2

Colonial Representations

Camus's plain style and unadorned reporting of social situations conceal rivetingly complex contradictions, contradictions unresolvable by rendering, as critics have done, his feelings of loyalty to French Algeria as a parable of the human condition.

– Edward W. Said[1]

The Stranger, a Novel of Denial

The Stranger by Albert Camus (1942) called into question religion, marriage, and the death penalty. Yet the form of 'philosophical' radicalism illustrated in the novel also carries within it a radical exclusion: the denial of the Algerian as a human being. This denial – which simultaneously amounts to an acceptance of colonial reality – takes the form of an indifference that is not explained but instead presented as an almost neutral fact, as an unquestionable given. Yet this assumption has rarely been identified or examined in a detailed and critical manner.

Critiques of The Stranger

In his critical book *Albert Camus*,[2] published in 1970, Conor Cruise O'Brien describes the plot of *The Stranger*, its setting, and its characters, as a representation of the colonial situation.

---

1   Edward W. Said, *Culture and Imperialism*, New York: Random House, 1994, 185.

2   Conor Cruise O'Brien, *Camus*, London: Faber and Faber, 1985.

He sees in it the manifestation of the hesitations and limitations of the conscience of the Western man when it comes to the colony.[3] For Edward Said, O'Brien's euphemistic way of referring to French imperialism and his conception of Algeria as a frontier of Europe reflect a refusal to criticize the colonial project and the role Camus's work plays within it: 'After exposing the link between Camus's most famous work and the colonial situation in Algeria, O'Brien absolves Camus.'[4]

The reaction of a prominent Camus specialist to O'Brien's book was very different from Said's. In a review entitled 'From One Mirage to Another, or the Traps of Symptomatic Literary Criticism',[5] André Abbou opens his critique by listing inaccuracies that, all things considered, hardly seem significant.[6] But, when O'Brien points out the anonymity of Arabs in *The Stranger* and their absence from *The Plague*, Abbou becomes genuinely indignant: 'As for the absence of Arabs in *The Plague*, why not relate it to the absence of Spaniards, Jews, and other religious or ethnic communities?'[7] The very mention of the absence or anonymity of Arabs strikes him as 'childish' and gives him 'vertigo'.[8] For Abbou, O'Brien's interpretation of *The Stranger* and *The Plague* can be explained by his Irish origins:

> O'Brien's interpretation of *The Stranger* and *The Plague* is the response of an Irishman, alienated and dominated by England, who projects everywhere the mark of his complexes and aversions. There are certainly, moreover, fruitful reflections to pursue on Irish emigrants in the United States who, once integrated into

---

3 Ibid., 27.

4 Said, *Culture and Imperialism*, 173.

5 André Abbou, 'D'un mirage l'autre ou les pièges de la critique littéraire symptomale', *La Revue des lettres modernes*, no. 6 (1972): 179–87.

6 For example, Abbou states 'Camus's first marriage was not "broken off" in 1936: there was a separation'; ibid., 180.

7 Ibid., 184.

8 Ibid.

the establishment, oppress – like other white communities – the black population.[9]

Abbou's nationalist conception of literary analysis is not tempered by what he considers Camus's only fault with regard to Algeria, namely forgetting that colonial oppression 'sometimes drives people to despair and to the decision to become masters of their destiny at any cost, without concern for the means or *the limits of their right*'.[10]

This frontal opposition to any critique of colonial representations in Camus's work is symptomatic of the broader denial that prevails in the most influential literary and political fields regarding France's colonial past. This denial serves to conceal what many in these fields believe: that the Algerians, in fighting to win their independence, had 'overstepped the limits of their rights'.

It is important to note that, several decades later, this denial remains fully operative. It is the same André Abbou who wrote the entry on *The Stranger* in the new edition (2006–8) of Camus's *Œuvres complètes*, which he coedited and was published by Gallimard. In the textual notes, his position – thirty years after his first article – regarding O'Brien remains unchanged. As for the anonymity of Arabs in the novel, Abbou – perhaps somewhat disingenuously – merely responds to the criticism by explaining that this anonymization is 'whatever it may seem, a mark of respect and consideration'.[11]

More recently, in January 2012, Michel Onfray entered the debate with a controversial biography of Albert Camus, in which no mention is made of the particular status of Arabs in *The Stranger*.[12] He nevertheless grants Camus the status of an 'anticolonialist thinker from his earliest years and throughout

---

9 Ibid., 186.

10 Ibid., my emphasis.

11 André Abbou, 'Notes sur le texte', in Camus, *Œuvres complètes*, vol. IV, no. 14, 1226.

12 Michel Onfray, *L'Ordre libertaire*, Paris: Flammarion, 2012.

the rest of his life'.[13] This directly contradicts Camus's public positions, which, as shown, were in no way favourable to independence. One need only recall his statement during the War of Independence, in 1958:

> The claim for Algerian national independence must be regarded in part as a manifestation of this new Arab imperialism, which Egypt, overestimating its strength, claims to lead, and which Russia is currently using for anti-Western strategic purposes. The fact that this demand is unrealistic does not prevent – quite the opposite – its strategic use.[14]

Onfray has never shied away from manipulation: the central section of his book features an image of Nazi soldiers executing opponents, placed directly above that of the corpse of a 'victim of the FLN'. The effect is to draw a parallel between Algerian independence fighters and the Nazis.

Onfray's book was nevertheless published by a prestigious press (Flammarion) and received favourable coverage from the major French media.[15] This quasi-official support stands in contrast to the gradual emergence of certain voices on the left that address the Algerian War of Independence without taboo: Daeninckx's novel *Murder for Memory* (1983) was followed by Sebbar's *The Seine Was Red* (1999); after Haneke's film *Hidden* (2005) came Bouchareb's *Days of Glory* (2006). But, for sharp and precise responses to Onfray's distortions and neocolonial bad faith, one must turn, instead, to Algerian criticism, notably the commentary by Mohammed Yefsah, which centres on the French biographer's ignorance:

---

13 Ibid., 26.

14 Camus, 'Algeria 1958', cited in *Algerian Chronicles*, 178.

15 See, for example, François Busnel, 'François Busnel a lu L'Ordre libertaire de Michel Onfray', *L'Express*, 18 January 2012; François Boscher, 'Michel Onfray rend justice à Camus', *Ouest-France*, 20 February 2012; Christophe Lucet, 'Albert Camus, le parcours d'un juste', *Sud-Ouest*, 20 January 2012.

For Onfray, Algerian intellectuals who criticize Camus have certainly and inevitably not read the novelist's works. They are even 'so-called intellectuals' who should 'free themselves from mental slavery', in the pay of the regime. If Onfray does not know this, it is time to inform him that Camus is taught in Algeria, that the regime has never banned any of his books, and that no official statement has ever been issued against him. An incalculable number of dissertations, university theses, and comparative literary studies have been devoted to him, from diverse and divergent perspectives. He should know that among the intellectuals who criticize Camus, some are even opponents of the Algerian regime. He forgets that Yasmina Khadra, a defender of Camus, is an official representative of an Algerian institution. He also forgets that these positions can be read in the columns of an Algerian newspaper, whereas in France none of the Algerian intellectuals he attacks are invited to express their views.[16]

Many Algerian intellectuals have gone beyond hagiography in their engagement with Camus and his work.[17] Let us conclude with the words of Mohamed Bouhamidi on 'the promoters of Camus, who have invented an unreal Camus. They want to turn him into a cause – that of a fantasized colonialism, humane and benevolent.'[18]

Colonial representations: Meursault's indifference and loyalty

The subversive challenges to Catholic morality (regarding mourning) and bourgeois morality (regarding marriage) in *The*

---

16   Mohammed Yefsah, 'L'imposture Onfray', in 'Réponses à Michel Onfray', available at ahmedbensaada.com. My translation.

17   A few are cited in this volume: Messaoud Benyoucef, Christiane Chaulet-Achour, Omar Merzoug.

18   Mohamed Bouhamidi, 'Faire de Camus la cause de la réhabilitation coloniale', *La Tribune*, 18 March 2010, in *Quand les Algériens lisent Camus*, Algiers: Casbah Éditions, 2014, 41. My translation.

Stranger coexist with a praxis – expressed through actions, through writing, and through omissions – of support for and loyalty to the agents of colonial exploitation.

This colonial doxa reduces the colonized to a subhuman being, foreign to the humanist values of metropolitan universalism. This denial of the Other was described as an error – more strategic than moral – by Guy de Maupassant a little over fifty years earlier, in one of his Algerian short stories:

> And I thought of this defeated people among whom we are encamped – or rather who are encamped among us ... upon whom we impose our laws, our regulations, and our customs, and of whom we know nothing – nothing at all, do you hear me.[19]

The acuity of this warning is confirmed by a reading of *The Stranger*. French contempt for Algerians is expressed in the novel through the author's distance from all Algerian characters, but also through the narrator's actions: Meursault acts against Algerians several times.

The Stranger recounts a news item, a case of pimping that turns into murder. The person from whom everything begins is a pied-noir pimp named Sintès. The surname matters: it is the maiden name of Camus's mother, Catherine Hélène Sintès. He is, in a sense, one of the family.

This pimp, Raymond Sintès, attempts to prostitute a young Algerian woman (unnamed in the narrative), who refuses. She is violently beaten, and the pimp is questioned by the police. Meursault helps Sintès in various ways, notably by providing the police with a false statement to clear him. The police, already largely indifferent to the fate of the young woman, subsequently lose interest in the case, which leads to several confrontations between, on the one hand, the victim's brother and his friends, and, on the other, Sintès and an enforcer

---

19 Guy de Maupassant, *Allouma, Contes et Nouvelles*, vol. II, Paris: Gallimard, 1979, 1104. My translation.

(Masson), along with Meursault. These confrontations ultimately end with the murder of the woman's brother, or one of his companions.

This fatal affair of morals undoubtedly offers another aspect of the rejection of bourgeois values – a morality according to which Meursault, as an office worker, should not associate with men from the underworld. This episode is therefore also meant, like Meursault's reactions to mourning, marriage, and work, to shock the bourgeois reader. Sintès and Meursault initially come together in their shared hatred of the 'cop'. Meursault recognizes Sintès as a full subject, as an equal – they are both outsiders to respectable morality, indifferent to public opinion.

Who is this character? An existential hero? A hard-boiled novel figure? An office clerk seeking thrills, shrugging off his jacket to become a small-town, racist white man? Racism is presented here as a marker meant to shock bourgeois propriety and tolerance. Meursault is a bourgeois anti-bourgeois. This overlapping of identities contrasts with the character of Sintès, who is not posturing. Meursault, by contrast, constantly inhabits an in-between position, mirroring the author himself: Albert Camus-Sintès.

Like Sintès, the anonymous characters whom Camus refers to simply as 'Arabs' do not change either, confined as they are to their subaltern positions. What we see here is an acceptance and faithful reproduction of the status of the colonized in French Algeria. For everything in *The Stranger* seems, in practice, to deny Algerians the status of human beings. First, there is a denial of identity: throughout the novel, Algerians are designated only by their 'race' – no surname, no given name is ever provided, which in a sense reduces them to extras. Physical descriptions, when they appear, are often derogatory (the Algerian nurse who appears at the beginning of the novel has a chancre). Second, there is a denial of speech, since no Algerian is a 'speaking' character – with the exception of the young woman whom Sintès attempts to prostitute, but no one listens to her.[20] Meursault feels no sympathy whatsoever for the young woman's ordeal; on the contrary, he shields her persecutor.

In *The Stranger*, colonialism is taken for granted. Yet even a cursory reading of the history of the conquest of Algeria – even one based on the correspondence of its conquerors (Bugeaud or Saint-Arnaud) or its ideologues (Tocqueville) – reveals an occupation of extraordinary brutality, founded on state racism and on systematic, planned massacres (notably the *razzias*, which involved destroying entire villages and killing – often through smoke suffocation – all inhabitants of fighting age).[21] France's colonization of Algeria was a dispossession that lasted more than a century, and from 1870 onwards Algeria was conceived as an integral part of France, not only in metropolitan minds but also administratively. In this context, Camus's outcry during his famous press conference in Stockholm, shortly after accepting the Nobel Prize for Literature – 'I believe in justice, but I will defend my mother before justice' – takes on a particular resonance.

What was presented as a Cornelian dilemma was in fact, as Messaoud Benyoucef lucidly wrote, 'the admission that he could imagine no status for his mother other than the one guaranteed to her by the oppression of a people'.[22] An involuntary confession whose roots can be found in the most violent character, the one most unjust towards Algerians: Raymond Sintès, who, as we have seen, is family. In this way, Camus's refusal of the historical movement towards decolonization – whose inevitability he understood – makes him a Baudelairean figure: the last great colonial writer, swimming against the current of History.

---

20 Albert Camus, *L'Étranger*, in *Œuvres complètes*, vol. I, Paris: Gallimard, 2006, 162.

21 Ageron, *Histoire de l'Algérie contemporaine*, 176–8. See also historian Hosni Kitoumi's crucial new book for an Algerian perspective: *Histoire, mémoire et colonisation*, Algiers: Chihab editions, 2025.

22 Messaoud Benyoucef, 'Fallait-il préférer sa mère à la justice ou affronter les ultras de l'OAS?', *Le Monde*, 10 January 2010, lemonde.fr.

Nature as an Escape from History

What strikes the reader in retrospect in *The Stranger* is the complete absence of any apparent motive for the murder. Meursault arrives at the crime scene without premeditation; this is not a matter of police procedure, nor a conventional mystery about the identity of the criminal. *The Stranger* runs counter to the expectations of the detective novel. So why does Meursault kill the young Algerian? At first glance, it is inexplicable. Even if the context presents Meursault as a man who might have had reasons to wish harm on the enemy of his friend, the pimp Raymond Sintès, the murder takes place after the fight.

Our hypothesis is that Meursault kills the Algerian because he interrupts and disturbs his communion with nature. As we have seen, Meursault does not inhabit the temporality of his era. This distance manifests itself both negatively and positively. On the negative side, it appears in everything related to society's organization of time: forgetting dates (mourning) or his mother's age, and an inability to project himself into the future (his refusal of promotion). By contrast, the pleasure he takes in going to the beach, in swimming, and in his relationship to the sun constitute a kind of sensual bond with nature that is one of the character's only motivations.

The sun that Meursault venerates throughout the novel functions as a symbol of this relationship to nature, which resembles a futile desire to escape human temporality. As Roland Barthes wrote in 1954, in '*The Stranger*, a Solar Novel': 'Meursault is a man bodily subjected to the sun, and I believe this submission must be understood in an almost sacred sense. [The sun] makes history.'[23] The human temporality that Meursault rejects is not merely that of passing days, but that of collective memory. Meursault seeks to avoid History just as he avoids recognizing

---

23 Roland Barthes, *Œuvres complètes*, vol. I, Paris: Le Seuil, 1993, 480.

the humanity of Algerians. This mirrors Camus's reluctance to inscribe the lives of French settlers within the historical process of invasions and repressions intrinsic to French colonization in Algeria.

According to Franco Cassano, the rejection of the Hegelian notion of History is fundamental to Camus's thought.[24] It gives way to a kind of veneration of nature – of the sun and the sea – that does not amount to a theory or an explanation of the world but, instead, directly replaces religion and the Enlightenment.[25] This relationship to an idealized, superior nature recurs frequently in Camus's work, notably in his final, unfinished novel *The First Man*:

> The Mediterranean divided two worlds within me: one where, in measured spaces, memories and names were preserved; the other where the desert wind erased the traces of men across vast expanses.[26]

What is at stake here is the erasure of Algeria and of Algerians, but also the advent of another moral scale, one in which human histories are rendered insignificant. This makes it possible to deny the past of the indigenous population by relativizing it, and to efface the recent past altogether. In this romantic conception, nature becomes a character in its own right – most strikingly in the murder scene in *The Stranger*: the day 'no longer advanced', it had 'dropped anchor in an ocean of seething metal'. What drives Meursault to commit the crime, to avoid turning back and to return to the beach hut? The sun: 'But the whole beach throbbing with sunlight pressed in behind me.'[27] He moves towards the Algerian in an attempt to

---

24 Franco Cassano, *Southern Thought and Other Essays on the Mediterranean*, New York: Fordham University Press, 2012, 210–13.

25 Ibid.

26 Albert Camus, *Le Premier homme*, in *Œuvres complètes*, vol. IV, 181. My translation.

27 Camus, *L'Étranger*, in *Œuvres complètes*, vol. I, 181.

escape the sun, even though he knows he cannot rid himself of it in that way. And then comes the unbearable moment: the Algerian appropriates the sun. He places it on the blade of his knife and takes symbolic possession of it by reflecting its glare back at Meursault. The appropriation of space – here, the beach – by the Arab constitutes a first violation. The intrusion of the Algerian into the relationship that Meursault (and Camus) maintains with the Algerian sun, into this synchronic, fusion-like bond with nature that allows one to repress and ignore the chronological reality of colonialism, constitutes a second violation. Symbolically, this incursion into a Garden of Eden reserved for the colonists is a cardinal sin. The Other is therefore put to death for having destabilized, by his very presence, the fantasy of a universe founded on his exclusion. This interpretation of the text corresponds to the colonial reality of which it is the reflection: in French Algeria, 'the behavioural code ... requires that an Arab yield to a European'.[28]

The Plague, or the Fear of Contagion

I believe in a united Europe, drawing strength from Latin America, and later – once the nationalist virus will have lost its strength – from Asia and from Africa.

– Albert Camus[29]

In January 1941, Camus was in Algeria, having returned from Lyon after the collapse of his employer, the popular daily *Paris-Soir*. Without steady work, he scraped by in Oran, a city he did not like. Recently married and penniless, he was forced to live with his in-laws, who were very attached to tradition;

---

28   Christiane Chaulet-Achour, *Albert Camus, Alger, L'Étranger et autres récits*, Biarritz: Séguier, 1999, 89. My translation.

29   Albert Camus, *Œuvres complètes*, vol. IV, Paris: Gallimard, 2008, 660. Response to a *Reconstruir* questionnaire, December 1959.

moreover, his mother-in-law was rather irascible. The city itself was ugly: 'There is no place that the people of Oran have not defiled with some hideous construction that should crush any landscape.' And yet his feelings were ambivalent: 'No one would think of writing about a city where nothing stimulates the mind, where ugliness has taken on a disproportionate role, where the past is reduced to nothing. And yet this is sometimes very tempting.'[30]

He gives in to temptation. *The Plague* would therefore be set in Oran, a city-character meant to represent France that Camus presents as eminently ordinary.

The opening lines reflect this desire for normalization: 'Oran is in fact an ordinary town, nothing more than a French prefecture on the Algerian coast.' The historical reality was quite different: Oran was strikingly atypical within occupied Algeria. In 1921, the Algerian population there accounted for only 12 percent of the inhabitants (while it represented nearly 90 percent across the country as a whole). But this imbalance was bound to reverse itself: in 1931, the number of Algerians in Oran had almost doubled, reaching 20 percent of the population; by 1954, 40 percent of Oran's inhabitants were Algerian.[31]

At the time of *The Plague*, Oran was therefore a city populated by a large majority of settlers. But it was a majority living on borrowed time. At the outset of the Second World War, this demographic shift was already under way. Oran was, in fact, at the forefront of a radical demographic transformation.

The deliberate omission of Algerians is therefore striking: this looming demographic reversal is transposed in the text into the appearance of a virus, a disease deadly to the European

---

30   Albert Camus, *Œuvres complètes*, vol. II, Paris: Gallimard, 2006, 918–19. What redeems Oran in Camus's eyes? The *creature*: 'For a certain breed of men, the creature – wherever she is beautiful – is a homeland with a thousand capitals', 919. My translation.

31   Charles-Robert Ageron, *Histoire de l'Algérie contemporaine*, vol. II: *De l'insurrection de 1871 au déclenchement de la guerre de libération*, Paris: Presses Universitaires de France, 1964, 473.

inhabitants of this supposedly ordinary city. In *The Plague*, no Algerian ever appears, to the point that Conor Cruise O'Brien spoke of an 'artistic final solution'.[32] One of the first scenes of the novel is ambiguous and confusing:

> On the afternoon of the same day, at the beginning of his consultation, Rieux received a young man who was said to be a journalist and who had already come by that morning. His name was Raymond Rambert ... He came straight to the point. He was investigating, for a major Paris newspaper, the living conditions of the Arabs and wanted information about their state of health. Rieux told him that this state was not good. But before going any further, he wanted to know whether the journalist could tell the truth.
>
> 'Certainly,' the other man said.
>
> 'I mean: can you deliver an unqualified condemnation?'
>
> 'Unqualified, no, I have to say I can't. But I suppose that such a condemnation would be unfounded.'
>
> Gently, Rieux said that indeed such a condemnation would be unfounded, but that in asking the question he was simply trying to find out whether Rambert's report could be without reservations or not.
>
> 'I can only accept a report without reservations. I therefore will not contribute to yours with my information.'[33]

Let us be clear: Rieux refuses to cooperate with an investigation into the living conditions of the 'Arabs' on the grounds that he does not want to work with someone who would at the outset refuse to conceive of a total condemnation of those living conditions – a total condemnation which, according to Rieux's own assertion, has no reason to exist in any case. The

---

32 'It is also surprising ... that commentators on Camus should have missed the significance of this artistic final solution of the problem of the Arabs in Oran', in Conor Cruise O'Brien, *Camus*, vol. I, London: Faber and Faber, 1985, 48–9.

33 Camus, *Œuvres complètes*, vol. II, 41. My translation.

doctor's perplexing and grandiloquent posture barely succeeds in concealing his unease: it strongly resembles the rhetorical techniques that Camus employed in order to try to camouflage his contradictions with regard to colonialism.

This sophism on the part of the doctor – who will turn out to be the narrator – reveals a desire to appear as a free and uncompromising character. Yet in practice it amounts to a refusal to contribute to an investigation into the living conditions of Algerians in Oran – Algerians who will never be seen in the novel. This is a different kind of procedure than in *The Stranger*: an organized omission; the reader is not even supposed to notice that the Algerians are not there. Kabyle writer Mouloud Feraoun, however, did notice, and wrote a letter to Camus concerning *The Plague*:

> I had regretted that among all these characters there was not a single indigenous person, and that Oran appeared in your eyes as nothing more than an ordinary French prefecture. Oh, This is not meant as a reproach! I simply thought that, if this gulf did not exist between us, you would have known us better, and felt able to speak of us with the same generosity as everyone else.[34]

The indigenous question is abruptly brushed aside; the two men change the subject: 'The doctor shook his hand and said there would be an interesting article to write about the number of dead rats being found in the city at the moment. "Ah!" exclaimed Rambert. "That interests me."' The substitution has taken place. Algerians will no longer be spoken of directly in *The Plague*.

One might therefore think this is a novel in which the plague serves as an allegory of the German occupation of France, giving this intra-European conflict a universal scope. I propose a different reading: the plague is not Germany or the Germans, but the resistance of the Algerian people to French

---

34 Mouloud Ferraoun, Lettre à Camus, mai 1951, in *Lettres à ses amis*, Paris: Le Seuil, 1969, 54. My translation.

occupation – a phenomenon that is intermittent yet inescapable, and which appears as a deadly disease from the settlers' point of view. A brief historical overview of these suppressed resistances is therefore necessary in order to grasp the extent of this settler repression, which periodically resurfaces with each new uprising.

In his *History of Contemporary Algeria*, Charles-Robert Ageron describes the origins of the occupation as follows: it was initially conceived as a temporary intervention, at a moment when the Bourbon monarchy was in crisis. The attack on Algiers 'was not part of the colonial policy of the Restoration. It was both an improvised expedient and a gesture of domestic politics, carried out by a government in difficulty seeking a show of prestige.'[35]

On 5 July 1830, under a false pretext, 35,000 French soldiers occupied Algiers. Initially, French military strategy consisted in forming an alliance with Emir Abd el-Kader against the Ottomans. A French general (Desmichels) allied himself with the Algerian leader, who had defeated the Turkish forces and their auxiliaries. Very quickly, however, Abd el-Kader's numerous victories over the Ottomans alarmed the French authorities, who then turned against him. For more than ten years, Abd el-Kader's troops repeatedly routed the French army. He controlled two capitals in Western Algeria, Tlemcen, and Mascara, as well as large portions of Algerian territory. The defeated General Bugeaud returned to the metropole in 1839. For France, Algeria was not an easy conquest – far from it.

Upon General Bugeaud's return in 1842, now convinced of the necessity of total war and backed by Paris, Abd el-Kader was forced to abandon his permanent bases and wage a guerrilla war that lasted until 1847, when he was captured and deported to the metropole. It is worth noting that Abd el-Kader – today a largely overlooked figure in France – was

---

35 Ageron, *Histoire de l'Algérie contemporaine (1830–1994)*, 6.

celebrated fifteen years later by Victor Hugo in *Les Châtiments* as a man both 'fierce and gentle', a 'fine soldier ... a fine priest', in striking contrast to Napoleon III, 'the shifty man of the Élysée'.[36]

In 1870, on the eve of the Franco-Prussian War, the French army was still presented as invincible, victorious in Crimea and in Italy, 'yet within a few weeks it was defeated on every battlefield [by the Prussian army]. The emperor and the marshals capitulated.'[37] A year later, in 1871, tens of thousands of Algerians rose up against the French army. This was the 'Kabyle insurrection', which lasted several months.

What emerges from this brief overview is that, throughout the occupation, the settlers were never safe from spontaneous revolts – each one shaking the military and civil edifice of the invaders. Consequently, the fear of a 'relapse' marked the consciousness of the pieds-noirs.

This view of the French colonial experience – fraught with obstacles and doomed to certain failure – resembles an existentialist conception of life: it will be short and will have only one certainty – its end. In this sense, each Algerian uprising acts as a reminder of the finite nature of the French Empire.

If there is a parallel to be drawn in *The Plague*, it is therefore not with the German occupation of France, but with the French occupation of Algeria. *The Plague* is the novel of a city with a European majority, the result of the ethnic cleansing carried out by Generals Bugeaud and de Lamoricière, ultimately supported by Tocqueville.[38]

The novel ends with a warning to the settlers: Doctor Rieux

---

36 Victor Hugo, *Œuvres poétiques*, vol. II, *Les Châtiments*, Paris: Gallimard, 1967, 72–3. My translation.

37 Charles-André Julien, *Histoire de l'Algérie contemporaine (1827–1871)*, vol. I, Paris: Presses Universitaires de France, 1964, 473.

38 'I believe that the laws of war authorize us to devastate the country': Alexis de Tocqueville, *Œuvres,* vol. I: *Travail sur l'Algérie,* Paris: Gallimard, 1991, 706.

looks on in disbelief at the festivities celebrating the end of the epidemic; he knows full well that the plague will return, that this victory is only temporary – in the same way that an uprising's repression will not prevent others from emerging with increasing frequency and ever greater force, until they alter the course of human history.

> Rieux remembered that this rejoicing was always under threat. For he knew what this jubilant crowd did not know, and *that can be read in books*: that the plague bacillus never dies or disappears, that it can remain dormant for decades ... that it waits patiently in bedrooms, cellars ... and that perhaps the day would come when, for the misfortune and *the instruction* of humankind, the plague would rouse its rats and send them forth to die in a happy city.[39]

This jubilant crowd, meant to evoke that of the liberation of Paris in the summer of 1944, could just as easily be the crowd of European settlers in Algeria who were celebrating in Algiers, with great pomp, the centenary of the invasion and occupation in 1930. We should also note the narrator's near certainty that the plague would return – a return that 'can be read in books': the appeal to knowledge confirms the colonists' worst fears. The History to come will be Hegelian; it will be the dramatic unfolding of the inevitable triumph of the oppressed, of slaves over their masters.

---

39 Camus, *Œuvres complètes*, vol. II, 248. Emphasis added.

3

Sartre and Camus, Inseparable

Circumstances have changed, the polemicists are dead, and two generations of writers have emerged since then. But this controversy is still relevant today. Every morning, the newspapers bring it up again, along with their share of disasters and the political and moral dilemmas in which they plunge us. The nearly thirty years that have passed have cleared the ground and swept away the debris.

– Mario Vargas Llosa, *Entre Sartre y Camus*[1]

Afterlives

In France today, among media intellectuals,[2] there are many former protégés of Sartre – figures whom he defended in the public sphere or before the courts when necessary.[3] They now constitute the old anti-Sartrean rearguard: through polemics and repetitive books, they have been repudiating their former master for nearly half a century. According to them, Sartre was a bad writer, an antisemite, a Stalinist, a collaborator, and an apologist for terrorism.

---

1   Mario Vargas Llosa, *Entre Sartre y Camus*, Puerto Rico: Ediciones Huracán, 1981, 10. My translation.

2   Bernard-Henri Lévy, the late André Glucksmann, Pascal Bruckner – just to name a few.

3   For example, in May 1970, Sartre testified at the trial of the Maoist leaders Le Dantec and Le Bris. See Annie Cohen-Solal, *Sartre, 1905–1980*, Paris: Gallimard, 1999, 795.

In this context, the break between Camus and Sartre is endlessly replayed – but now as farce – by way of competing biographies: that of Bernard-Henri Lévy, who does not hesitate to rewrite history by imagining a Sartre cleansed of his anti-colonialism, or that of Michel Onfray, who deifies Camus while transforming Sartre into a collaborator.[4] For the former, Sartre's great crime was to have theorized (with Frantz Fanon), and then encouraged, anti-colonial counter-violence (the 'smoking gun' being the preface to *The Wretched of the Earth*); for the latter, the true criminals are the colonized, guilty of having dared to use violence in order to liberate themselves. For both, their condemnation of anti-colonial counter-violence alone is what they believe unites them with Camus. Yet what, for Camus, was a long personal tragedy – torn as he was between colony and metropole – is, for Onfray and Lévy, nothing more than the automatic reflex of intellectuals organically tied to the French state and its interests. The Camus they create is an indispensable element in their pro-colonial and anti-communist stagings. Camus is Good; Sartre is Evil. The glorification of Camus has the further advantage of allowing them to erase Sartre and his critique of French and American imperialism. All these attacks demonstrate just how central Sartre remains to the French intellectual debate, even if only as a negative reference. For these pseudo-philosophers – the kind Paul Nizan famously dubbed 'guard dogs' of the system – Camus is an 'anti-Sartre agent': invoking him makes it possible to combine the aura of commitment with the defence of neocolonialism, as a counterpoint to the excessively dangerous analyses of his elder.

Another perspective on the relationship between the two men, and on their respective political trajectories during the German occupation and the postwar period, is therefore necessary.

---

4 Michel Onfray, *L'Ordre libertaire*, Paris: Flammarion, 2012, 224–30.

A Friendship That Ended Badly?

Rather than the familiar story of a friendship that ends badly, it is more accurate to conceive of this relationship as the gradual unveiling of an irreducible antagonism. Sartre tried, unsuccessfully, to win Camus over to his views, but he had underestimated the importance of Camus's ideological invariant as a European of Algeria. It is this unexamined constant – one Camus initially concealed, most of all from himself – that Sartre would unwittingly expose.

Even before they met, their relationship was already ambivalent. Each, in turn, acted as the other's critic. Camus opened hostilities: his review of *Nausea* in the 'literary salon' of *Alger républicain* (October 1938) is more than ambiguous. It contains many laudatory remarks, but the negative assessments are unquestionably more detailed and more forceful. For this young critic (Camus was twenty-four), *Nausea* – one of the great philosophical novels of the twentieth century, whatever one may think of its author – was 'not a work of art'.[5] The fault lay, he argued, in the 'clumsy' juxtaposition of the novelistic and the philosophical. The synthesis is unsuccessful: the resulting 'imbalance' produces a sense of 'discomfort' that 'prevents the reader's full engagement'.[6]

Camus wrote this article during his most romantic period: in his private journals as well as in his essays, he proclaims the superiority of sensations over ideas and his implacable disdain for all 'attempts at explanation'. It is also possible that Camus felt a form of class resentment towards Sartre, who, a rising star of French literature and a very bourgeois child prodigy, had passed through the École normale supérieure, an institution which Camus had been unable to attend.

---

5 Albert Camus, 'Le Salon de lecture d'Alger républicain', in *Œuvres complétes*, vol. I, 794–5.

6 Ibid., 795.

Nearly four years later, it was Sartre's turn, with his 'Explanation of *The Stranger*', published in *Les Cahiers du Sud* (February 1943). The piece reads like a genuine lesson from teacher to pupil: 'M. Camus shows a certain coquettishness in citing texts by Jaspers, Heidegger, and Kierkegaard, which he does not always seem to understand very well.'[7] There can be little doubt that this remark must have struck home. In fact, Camus – who had repeated his philosophy year for health reasons – is described as a plagiarist by his quasi-official biographer Olivier Todd: 'To give more density to [what would today correspond to his master's thesis], he plunders from the experts … frequently forgetting to cite his sources.'[8] Moreover Sartre mocks the author of *The Myth of Sisyphus*, who 'talks a great deal … rambles even, and yet he confides to us his love of silence.'[9] Succinctly, Sartre lays out Camus's notion of the absurd: 'both a state of affairs and the lucid awareness that certain people acquire of that state'. And he goes on: 'Here we find the same shift in meaning as when one calls "swing" a youth that dances the swing.'[10]

Sartre's syntheses impressed the young Frenchman from Algeria, who confided in his mentor Jean Grenier in a letter: 'He sheds light on what I wanted to do.'[11] He added a complaint that seems particularly telling to us: 'Why this acidic tone?'[12] In another letter dated 11 March 1943 – one month before his first meeting with Sartre – Camus wrote to Francis Ponge that he had been told that 'Sartre does not like my essay

---

7   Jean-Paul Sartre, 'Explication de *L'Étranger*', *Situations I, février 1938 – septembre 1944*, Paris: Gallimard, 2010, 127–46.

8   Olivier Todd, *Albert Camus, une vie*, Paris: Gallimard, 1999, 142.

9   Sartre, 'Explication de *L'Étranger*', 127.

10   Ibid., 27.

11   Albert Camus and Jean Grenier, *Correspondence, 1932–1960*, Paris: Gallimard, 1981, 8. My translation.

12   Ibid.

at all'.[13] Even before they met, the mood was set, and it was bittersweet.

Yet, when the two writers met in person for the first time, in occupied Paris, on the occasion of the premiere of *The Flies* in June 1943, the atmosphere was rather cordial. Later, they certainly felt affection for one another and often met in cafés – one of the few heated places in Paris under the Occupation – to talk, drink, and joke. Camus nevertheless wrote at the time to Grenier that, 'despite appearances, I do not feel very much in common either with the work or with the man. But seeing those who are against him, one must be with him.'[14] Sartre, for his part, was particularly fond of Camus, at first almost as a curiosity: his frankness and his humour contrasted with his polished prose, but also with his appearance, which led his Parisian friends often to describe him as overdressed. If he caught sight of a woman he found attractive, he would immediately stop speaking, stop listening, and stare ostentatiously at the object of his attention. Ten years later, the protagonist of *The Fall*, Clamence, boasted that he preferred chatting with an attractive woman to having a conversation with Einstein. In the early days, Sartre and his partner Simone de Beauvoir met with Camus mainly for diversion; they rarely shared long, studious conversations – the outings were boozy, the discussions lively.

In his texts written during the Occupation, Sartre flatters Camus by citing him as *the* reference on the absurd. At this stage, it is clear that Sartre wanted to win Camus over to his point of view, and this tendency grew stronger in the following years, up to 1946. Sartre's personal relationships often overlapped with political, and militant, affinities. This was not the case with Camus. He explains his way of seeing things to

---

13   Albert Camus and Francis Ponge, *Correspondence, 1941–1957*, Paris: Gallimard, 2013, 43.

14   Albert Camus, letter to Jean Grenier, *Correspondance*, 99. According to Grenier, there was talk at the time of punishing Sartre for his play *The Flies* by placing him on leave from public teaching.

Ponge – who was then close to the Communist Party – in the form of a warning: 'I cannot live in a world where friendship itself serves tactics.'[15]

Yet, at the time of these first contacts, there was still a common enemy, one that brought them together almost in spite of themselves: if there was friendship, it was a 'national friendship that excused everything in advance in each person, provided that he hated the Nazis',[16] as Sartre described it in his portrait of Maurice Merleau-Ponty. And, as we shall see, this anti-Nazism manifested itself concretely in Sartre as soon as he returned from the prisoner-of-war camps, in April 1941.

Sartre, Resistance Intellectual

To better understand the two philosophers' divergent trajectories, let us examine Sartre's path during the Occupation. The resistance group Socialism and Freedom,[17] of which Sartre was one of the leaders, was unable to do very much, caught as it was between the Communist Party and the Gaullists. Its actions were limited – for example, its members wrote leaflets – translated into German – urging occupying soldiers to refuse to fight and left them in the subway cars reserved for Germans. Sartre started writing a constitution for a future socialist France, freed from the Nazis. Much has been said about this group – inept to the point of amateurism – especially by former members such as Merleau-Ponty or Nathalie Sarraute. But the fact remains that it existed for nearly a year, and that some of its members were arrested and deported. Sartre genuinely risked his life by committing himself to the Resistance before even the French Communist Party did, and before many intellectuals who

---

15   Albert Camus, letter to Francis Ponge, *Correspondance*, 94.

16   Jean-Paul Sartre, 'Merleau-Ponty', in *Situations VI, May 1958–October 1964*, Paris: Gallimard, 2020, 222. My translation.

17   Annie Cohen-Solal, 'Socialisme et liberté', in *Sartre*, 291–318.

would later, at the time of liberation, be labelled great resisters, sometimes even despite themselves. Sartre and Beauvoir also undertook a bicycle journey, in the summer of 1940, through Southern France in an attempt to persuade André Gide, André Malraux, and André Meyer (Blum's successor) to join their small group – all of whom declined, more or less directly. After the dissolution of Socialism and Freedom in the spring of 1942, Sartre's commitment became more strictly intellectual, in the manner of Jean Paulhan or Michel Leiris; he published texts hostile to collaboration that nonetheless managed to pass censorship.[18]

One of these, an article titled '*Moby-Dick* by Herman Melville, More Than a Masterpiece, a Monument',[19] now serves as the supposed 'proof' of Sartre's alleged collaboration in the eyes of some of his detractors.[20] It was published in *Comœdia*, and it is often pointed out that this cultural review was authorized by the occupying regime. What is mentioned less often is that neither Sartre nor Camus contributed to the highly influential *Nouvelle Revue française*, edited by the notorious collaborator Pierre Drieu la Rochelle and published by Gallimard – unlike many major writers of the period: André Gide, Henry de Montherlant, Marcel Jouhandeau, Jean Giono.

That famous article on *Moby Dick* is not merely an enthusiastic analysis of Herman Melville's novel (an author from a country at war with the Axis), but also a full-blown attack on Giono, a collaborator. Sartre targets him by calling him a 'minor, rural little prophet', in contrast to Melville, the 'great prophet'. He portrays Giono as a 'village notary' incapable of grasping the 'formidable monument'[21] that is *Moby Dick*. The

---

18   Cohen-Solal, *Sartre*, 795; Cohen-Solal, 'Socialisme et liberté', 291–318.

19   Sartre, *Situations I*, 121–46.

20   Most notably Gilbert Joseph, *Une si douce Occupation*, Paris: Albin Michel, 1991, as well as Michel Onfray in *L'Ordre libertaire*, 226–8.

21   Sartre, *Situations I*, 121–46.

aim is to humiliate one of the Vichy regime's favourite authors, who continuously praised that 'land that does not lie'.

That is not all. His play *The Flies* is a veiled homage to the young communist resisters who were the first to fight Wehrmacht officers and soldiers in occupied France.[22] Orestes, the son of King Agamemnon, symbolizes one of these early resisters. The entire play is an exhortation to fight against defeatism and the pervasive Pétainist culture of guilt. It thrilled those opponents of the regime who were able to attend a performance during the Occupation. Among them were Gilles Deleuze, Michel Leiris,[23] Michel Tournier,[24] Maurice Nadeau,[25] and Resistance leader Daniel Cordier.[26] Collaborationist commentators were not mistaken about the meaning of Sartre's words either: negative, even hostile reviews were numerous – there was even talk of striking Sartre from the rolls of the national education system.[27]

Sartre then joined the National Committee of Writers (CNE), a clandestine resistance organization that approved the staging of *The Flies*. He wrote several articles for *Les Lettres françaises*,

---

22   Sartre's support for young Communists who, through acts of urban guerrilla warfare, attacked soldiers and officers of the Wehrmacht – and the brutal crackdown that followed – lies at the heart of the French political divide over the stance to adopt towards the Resistance. None other than Jean-Marie Le Pen, in his *Memoirs*, invokes the severity of Nazi repression in an attempt to justify collaboration with the Nazi occupier.

23   'Saw yesterday, for the second time, Sartre's *The Flies*', letter of 20 June 1943, in *Journal 1922–1989*, Paris, Gallimard: 1992, 383.

24   Tournier went to see *The Flies* with Deleuze: Michel Tournier, *Romans suivi de Le Vent Paraclet*, Paris: Gallimard, 2017, 1420–1.

25   'I attended the first performance of *The Flies* ... the "collaborators" were not fooled ... Sartre's true intentions were perceived', in Maurice Nadeau, *Grâces leurs soient rendues*, Paris, Albin Michel, 1990, 59–60.

26   Daniel Cordier, '*The Flies* Is an Act of Resistance', in *La Victoire en pleurant, Alias Caracalla 1943–1946*, Paris: Gallimard, 2021, 32–4.

27   Camus, letter to Grenier, *Correspondance*, 98.

a clandestine publication, including a pamphlet in April 1943 against the collaborationist director of the *Nouvellle Revue Française*: 'Drieu la Rochelle, or Self-Hatred'. Jacques Lecarme, a preeminent specialist in Sartre, emphasizes the singularity of this short text:

> He was also quite literally the only one, in the meagre columns of this clandestine periodical [*Les Lettres françaises*] – which upheld the honour of a culture – to denounce Drieu's antisemitism … In this periodical the subject of antisemitism was so taboo that one never spoke of the deportation of Jews, only of that of the Resistance fighters … Sartre therefore did not wait for the Liberation to condemn racism by targeting the single truly formidable writer of the collaboration, and nothing is more foolish than the accusations that Sartre did not resist. Who, then, did better as a writer?[28]

Sartre did not stop there. In 1943, he made a second attempt to set up a clandestine group. To do so, he contacted Daniel Cordier, a leader of the Gaullist resistance and right-hand man to Jean Moulin, who coordinated the activity of armed underground groups between France and London. In his memoirs, Cordier recalls meeting with Sartre during the Occupation, and writes about his enthusiasm and his combativeness, and specifically, his requests:

> We are determined to plunge into action, but we need material assistance in our fight: blowing up trucks and trains, killing Germans … In short, resisting authentically. But we want to keep clear of all politics, to liberate France without playing into the hands of either the Communists or the Gaullists.
>
> I myself write articles for *Les Lettres françaises*, but what we want to invent is a group that carries out military actions against the occupier while at the same time functioning as a group of

---

28 Jacques Lecarme, *Drieu la Rochelle ou le bal des maudits*, Paris: Presses universitaires de France, 2001, 284. My translation.

reflection preparing the post-Liberation period, something like an 'intellectual commando'. I would like to introduce you to a few friends and get your opinion and your support.[29]

Sartre needed Cordier's logistical support. Cordier, aware of the dangers involved in a clandestine network made up of well-known writers, neither contradicted Sartre outright nor put him in touch with his networks. He nevertheless retained the highest esteem for him, for his talent and his courage. (Maurice Nadeau, in his *Literary Memoirs*, also recounts his exchanges with Sartre during the Occupation and his participation in a clandestine meeting of Socialism and Freedom.[30])

Need it be said again? Sartre was never, in any sense, a collaborator: according to Robert Paxton, one of the foremost specialists of the Occupation period, there is not the slightest doubt on this point.[31] Sartre's commitment to the Resistance was authentic, and he took genuine risks.

Camus, 'The Reasons for the Delay'

Camus's past as a member of the Resistance is today one of the least controversial aspects of his biography: he is said to have been a heroic – if discreet – member of the Resistance, and this from the very outset. The historical reality is more nuanced, according to Camus himself.

Even before the Occupation, during the 'Phony War' (between September 1939 and May 1940), Pascal Pia and Albert Camus – journalists and editorialists at the daily *Alger républicain* and then at *Le Soir républicain* – vigorously expressed their opposition to the war. This position was not appreciated by the authorities, who censored many of Camus's articles on the subject. On 6 November 1939 – two months

---

29 Cordier, *La Victoire en pleurant*, 31–2. My translation.
30 Nadeau, *Grâces leurs soient rendues*, 56–9.
31 Conversation with the author.

after France and Britain declared war on Germany – Camus signed an article in *Le Soir républicain* entitled 'Our Position'.[32] In it, he argued that negotiations were the only way to 'strip Hitler of the deep reasons for his prestige'.[33] For Camus, the Führer's popularity stemmed from the Treaty of Versailles. He wrote that some of Hitler's demands were 'legitimate'[34] and, although he condemned the invasions of Czechoslovakia and Poland, he did not believe they justified a war: in his view, it would have been necessary to 'yield in time' on certain demands and to reclaim those countries during any future negotiations: 'We believe that this conflict could have been avoided and can still be brought to a halt to the satisfaction of all.'[35]

The position taken by Camus and Pia – appeasement towards Hitler – became increasingly difficult to defend; amid a rise in patriotism, they were gradually isolated. In September 1939, *Alger républicain*, much of whose pacifist editorials were censored, became *Le Soir républicain*, which was itself banned in January 1940.

Camus found himself unemployed. Thanks to Pia's contacts, he joined *Paris-Soir*, a popular daily. He then lived in Paris, in a small hotel room in Montmartre. After the arrival of German troops in June, *Paris-Soir* moved to the unoccupied zone, to Lyon (after passing through Clermont-Ferrand and Bordeaux). Camus asked his fiancée, Francine Faure, to join him there; they were married in Lyon in December 1940. It was a simple wedding: Pia and the newspaper's workers served as witnesses and were the only attendees. Shortly thereafter, because paper rationing limited the daily's revenues, Camus was laid off once again. With no professional prospects, he reluctantly returned to Algeria to live with his in-laws in Oran. A year and a half

---

32 Camus, *Œuvres complètes*, vol. I, articles published in *Le Soir républicain*, 768–70. My translation.
33 Ibid., 770.
34 Ibid., 769.
35 Ibid., 770.

later, still without stable employment and with his health deteriorating, Camus decided – on medical advice – to return to France to spend some time in the mountain air and attempt to recover. In August 1942, he stayed in a small hamlet near Saint-Étienne, Le Panelier. Camus had planned to return to Francine in Algeria. But, after the American landings in North Africa on 11 November 1942, the German army invaded the unoccupied zone: lines of communication between France and Algeria were cut. 'Like rats',[36] Camus wrote in his private journal that very day, to express his frustration upon learning of this unexpected confinement.

As a result, Albert and Francine were separated, by force of circumstances, until her return to Paris in September 1944. He spent the summer of 1943 at Le Panelier. He was bored, disliked the company of the villagers, and missed Algeria. He devoted most of his time to working on his second novel, *The Plague*, interspersed with visits to Lyon, Saint-Étienne, and, more rarely, Paris. Although during the summer of 1943 he learned that Pascal Pia and Francis Ponge were involved in Resistance activities – consisting mainly of publishing small clandestine leaflets – Camus did not take part in their activities:

> He was doubtless not unaware of his friends' activities, but his serious health problems and his deep desire to return to Algeria did little, at that point, to encourage him to join them.[37]

According to both Patrick McCarthy and Yves Marc Ajchenbaum[38] (who cite Pascal Pia), Camus did not join the Resistance until December 1943 or January 1944. His two principal biographers, Herbert Lottman and Olivier Todd, confirm this late engagement.

---

36   Camus, *Œuvres complètes*, vol. II, 966. My translation.

37   Maurice Weyembergh, 'Notice', in *Œuvres complètes*, vol. II, 1130.

38   Albert Camus, Letter to Pascal Pia, *Correspondance 1939–1947*, Paris: Fayard-Gallimard, 2000, xxi.

Yet, from the immediate postwar period onwards, people close to Camus circulated the idea that he had joined the Resistance in 1942, or even earlier. One example among many of these inaccuracies can be found in the first edition of Camus's *Complete Works*, edited by his friend Roger Quilliot and published by Gallimard (1962): in the chronology at the beginning of the volume, under the year 1942, in the 'summer' section, one reads:

> Although he was not very forthcoming about his life as a resister, no doubt out of modesty and nostalgia, it seems that this was when he made contact … with the *Combat* network and the Liberation Nord movement, through Pascal Pia.[39]

More than forty years later, in the second edition of the *Complete Works* (2006), the ambiguity remains. It is no longer claimed that Camus joined the Resistance in 1942; this time, the date of May 1943 is given. Since Camus's false papers are dated May 1943, the author of the notes in this new edition sees this as confirmation of the moment of his engagement in the Resistance: 'A false identity card issued in the name of Albert Mathé, dated 20 May 1943, proves that by that date he was already well engaged in the Resistance.'[40] Yet, ten years earlier, Todd had specified that the card was backdated: May 1943 was chosen because the civil registry records for that month 'had temporarily disappeared', and therefore, 'in the event of arrest', the card 'could withstand interrogation'.[41]

Far from being a futile quarrel over chronological details, these inaccuracies deserve to be noted insofar as they help sustain a legend: that of Camus as an early resister who, out of modesty, remained silent about his engagement. This is not

---

39   Roger Quilliot, 'Biographie', in Albert Camus, *Théatre, récits, Nouvelles*, Paris: Gallimard, 1962, xxxiii.

40   Jacqueline Lévi-Valensi, 'Articles publiés dans *Combat* clandestin', in Camus, *Œuvres complètes*, vol. II, 14.

41   Todd, *Albert Camus, une vie*, 470. My translation.

the case, as we have seen. Camus initially held pacifist positions and hesitated at length before joining the Resistance. Camus's documented resistance activity therefore consisted primarily of writing his four letters (two of which were published between January and August 1944 in clandestine newspapers), as well as short articles and the chapter on Kafka in *The Myth of Sisyphus*, which he chose not to send to Gallimard in order to avoid antisemitic censorship. The most important writings of this period, however, are *Letters to a German Friend*.[42]

These are not really letters, but, rather, monologues addressed to an imaginary German 'friend' who speaks little and only through Camus (a technique used again years later in his novel *The Fall*). In the first text, 'Letter to a German Who Was My Friend', Camus explains 'the reasons for the delay': by this he means, more generally, the delay in France's response to the German invasion. For Camus, this delay originated in the search for a raison d'être. He advances the notion of an enlightened patriotism that seeks justifications – beyond mere nationalism – for going into battle. The French, he suggests, were suspicious of valour: 'But we still had to overcome this suspicion with which we regarded heroism. I know – you believe us to be strangers to heroism. You are wrong.'[43] This, he argues, is why France lost and why, after the defeat, so few resisted immediately. It is not impossible to see in these passages a justification of his own trajectory and his initial pacifism.

In the most recent edition of the *Complete Works*, the letter is dated July 1943 without further comment; in the critical apparatus, the year 1943 is given for its clandestine publication in *La Revue libre*. Consultation of the Bibliothèque nationale's website yields the exact publication date: February 1944.[44]

---

42 Albert Camus, 'Lettres à un ami allemand', in *Œuvres complètes*, vol. II, 9–29.

43 Ibid., 11.

44 gallica.bnf.fr/ark:/12148/bpt6k8784752?rk=21459;2#; the first issue of the review was published in 1943.

In the second letter, the delay in entering the Resistance is described as follows: 'that detour we took in search of our reasons, that delay imposed on us by our anxiety about our own legitimacy'.[45] Camus situates this inactivity at the beginning of the war; it took three years to reconcile nationalism with the pursuit of fairness and justice:

> We formed an idea of our country that placed it in its proper position, among other forms of greatness – friendship, humanity, happiness, our desire for justice ... We waited patiently until things became clear, and in misery and pain we obtained the joy of being able to fight at once for everything we loved.[46]

In a third letter, Camus undertakes a defence of the word 'Europe', which he sees as sullied by its association with Nazism. He asserts that Germany began to regard Europe as a land of conquest 'from the day you [the Germans] lost Africa'[47] (addressing his imaginary German friend). It is worth noting that, in many respects, Nazi Germany treated France as a colony during the Occupation, and that, at the time, the French – Camus among them – living under German domination were never objectively closer to the living conditions of Algerians under French rule. This is the point made by the scholar Omar Merzoug, who also underscores the contradiction of a Camus unwilling to grasp that 'Algerian patriots could have taken up for themselves his writings of 1944–45'.[48]

---

45 'Lettre à un ami allemand', 14.
46 Ibid., 15–16.
47 Ibid., 21.
48 *L'itinéraire politique d'Albert Camus*, in *Quand les Algériens lisent Camus*, Algiers: Casbah Éditions, 2014, 175–6. My translation.

Camus, Editorialist of the Resistance

In the immediate postwar period, Camus appeared as one of the spokesmen of the Resistance. The titles of his editorials from the summer of 1944 for the newspaper *Combat* read like rallying cries – lyrical declarations about France and its past, present, and future course: 'The Blood of Freedom',[49] 'The Night of Truth',[50] 'The Time of Contempt'.[51] In these columns he justified – and even glorified – liberating violence; he was indeed one of the major voices of the Resistance. He is often assumed to have been one of its leaders – for example, by being credited with the title of editor-in-chief of *Combat*. In his *Memoirs*, Raymond Aron, at the time a journalist for the paper, clarifies Camus's status:

> The head of this team [at *Combat*], contrary to common opinion, was never Albert Camus; it was Pascal Pia, an exceptional figure whose visible existence and public trajectory give no hint of what he was or what he might have done.[52]

Even before the end of the war, it was deemed essential to construct a collective fiction that would preserve at least the appearance of national unity. This is how the acts of resistance of André Malraux, Roger Martin du Gard, and Camus himself came to be overstated.

Today, this instrumentalization of the Occupation continues, albeit in a different form, since the ideological imperatives are no longer the same. Because Sartre's work too clearly reminds France of its colonial past, it has now become necessary to discredit him at all costs. From the 1990s onwards, a media and academic consensus has portrayed him as a quasi-collaborator with a purportedly far less honourable trajectory than the figure elevated in his place.

---

49 *Combat*, 24 August 1944.
50 *Combat*, 25 August 1944.
51 *Combat*, 30 August 1944.
52 Raymond Aron, *Mémoires*, Paris: Julliard, 1983, 208–9. My translation.

At a Distance from Existentialism

In the euphoria of the immediate postwar period, the two men appeared closer than ever. On behalf of *Combat*, Camus commissioned Sartre to write a series of articles on the liberation of Paris ('A Stroller in Insurgent Paris', seven pieces published between 22 August and 4 September), and also invited him to travel to the US as the newspaper's correspondent – a role Sartre would in fact assume during the first three months of 1945.

In October 1945, Sartre delivered his now-famous lecture on existentialism, published a year later as *Existentialism Is a Humanism*.[53] Existentialism was then in vogue, and Sartre and Beauvoir were its embodiment; Camus too – very much against his will.

During this period, both the French and international press most often portrayed this trio as two masters and their disciple. The deleterious effects of this narrative on Camus's psyche have likely not been sufficiently considered: he was adamant that he not be regarded as Sartre's disciple and took care to explain to all his interlocutors that he was in no sense an existentialist. But to no avail. Very few people distinguished between Camus's absurd and Sartre's existentialism. Camus was frequently described as an existentialist (as he still is today), a characterization that irritated him to the point of prompting him to take up his pen to reject this affiliation, with varying degrees of vehemence.

So, when a highly respected critic wrote that '*Caligula* ... is nothing more than an illustration of Mr. Sartre's existentialist principles', Camus's reply was swift: 'I am beginning to be a little (only a little) irritated by the constant confusion that implicates me in existentialism.'[54] His response unfolds

---

53   Jean-Paul Sartre, *L'Existentialisme est un humanisme*, Paris: Gallimard, 1996.

54   Albert Camus, 'Lettre à Monsieur le directeur de la NEF', in *Théâtre, Récits, Nouvelles*, 1745–6.

in three parts: first, *Caligula* was written in 1938, well before the publication of *Being and Nothingness*; second, *The Myth of Sisyphus* was written 'against existentialist philosophies';[55] and, third, he did not have sufficient faith in reason to belong to any system of thought. Despite this clarification (and many others), the confusion persisted. During his trip to New York in June 1946, for example, Camus answered the perennial question from a journalist, this time with a touch of irony: 'No, I am not an existentialist. Sartre and I are always surprised to see our two names linked. We are considering publishing an announcement in which the undersigned will affirm that they have nothing in common.'[56]

Out of this frustration was born his play styled *L'Impromptu des philosophes*.[57] Camus's resentment towards Sartrean existentialism ran so deep that in 1947 he wrote – hiding behind the pseudonym Antoine Bailly – a one-act play featuring a certain Monsieur Néant (Mister Nothingness, obviously echoing Sartre's *Being and Nothingness*), 'well known in Paris', who 'can do nothing with his two hands', and who carries under his arm a 'new gospel of which he is the apostle'.[58] Monsieur Vigne, a provincial pharmacist recently converted by Monsieur Néant, urges his son-in-law to practise 'pederasty' so that the discomfort it provokes will allow him to become conscious of his own existence. This is followed by homophobic wordplay on 'the love of man'. Sartre's existentialism is also presented as undermining patriarchal hierarchies: the disciple's daughter is encouraged to give birth to her child before marriage. Camus's anti-communism likewise resurfaces in a passage in which Monsieur Néant urges Monsieur Vigne to vote Communist: 'You will proclaim your love of freedom and at the same time

---

55 Ibid., 1746.

56 Ibid.

57 Albert Camus, *L'Impromptu des philosophes,* in *Œuvres complètes,* vol. II, 769–91. My translation.

58 Ibid., 772.

vote for those who wish to abolish it.'[59] The play gives voice to bourgeois and clerical common sense against what it presents as the most dangerous of Parisian intellectual fashions. And all ends well: the director of an asylum arrives to retrieve Monsieur Néant, an escaped patient, and order is restored. This theatrical project – hard to imagine it being staged in 1947 – offers a glimpse of the extent of Camus's animosity towards Sartre and existentialism and hints at his political outlook.

For Camus, Sartre was an antagonist, an unsurpassable point of reference against whom he would measure himself for nearly his entire life. The climax of this duel – this time on a far more explicitly political terrain – came in October 1957, several years after their break (they had not spoken directly since the spring of 1952). Camus was then at the height of his fame. During the press conference following his Nobel Prize acceptance speech, and as the Battle of Algiers was raging, he was questioned by an Algerian student about why he supported Eastern Europeans more readily than Algerians and pressed to publicly justify his stance – never before so directly stated – against independence and in favour of colonialism. To do so, he invoked his mother. His response was summarized in *Le Monde*: 'I believe in justice, but I will defend my mother before justice.'[60] Though the exact phrasing – 'if that is justice, I prefer my mother'[61] – differs, the admission is the same. To join the Resistance or to care for one's mother: this is a well-known Sartrean dilemma. Camus's statement in Stockholm could be heard as a public response to this dilemma. It directly echoed the crucial example from Sartre's 29 October 1945 lecture, 'Existentialism Is a Humanism', in which he describes existentialism as the awareness of an anxiety-inducing freedom that obliges us to make our decisions alone. He illustrates his notion of responsibility with an anecdote: that of a young man during

---

59 Ibid.
60 Camus, *Œuvres complètes*, vol. IV, 289. My translation.
61 Ibid., 1405.

the Occupation who comes to see his teacher (none other than Sartre himself) to ask for advice about a dilemma that is tearing him apart – should he attempt to join the Resistance or stay to care for his ailing mother? 'He found himself confronted with two very different kinds of action: one concrete and immediate, but addressed only to a single individual; the other addressed to an infinitely broader whole, a national collectivity.' Sartre refuses to advise the student:

> Whom should one love as a brother, the fighter or the mother? Which is the greater utility: the vague one of fighting within a collective, or the precise one of helping a specific person to live? Who can decide this in advance? No one. No written morality can say.[62]

Sartre leaves his student alone: 'You are free, choose – that is, invent.'[63] It is by explicitly invoking one of the most famous passages of the Sartrean corpus that Camus announced his existential choice in favour of the essentialism of his family, against Algerian independence. Sartre, therefore, appears, consciously or not, to be Camus's absolute point of reference.

The first major break between Camus and Sartre occurred in December 1946, just before the Indochina War, during a party. Camus violently reproached Merleau-Ponty for justifying the Stalinist trials. His anger was such that Jacques-Laurent Bost and Sartre had to intervene, then run after Camus as he stormed out. According to Sartre, it was a sentence from *Humanism and Terror* that lit the fuse: 'There is no room for neutral or indifferent actions; even silence plays its part, and the transitions from intention to act, from self to others, from opposition to betrayal, are imperceptible.'[64] Once again, it was

---

62 Sartre, *L'Existentialisme est un humanisme*, 42.

63 Ibid., 43.

64 Maurice Merleau-Ponty, *Humanisme et terreur* cited in Jean-Paul Sartre, *Les Mots et autres écrits autobiographiques*, n. 46, 1590. My translation.

the injunction to 'enter History' that provoked Camus's ire towards his 'German friend'. Following this dispute, Sartre and Camus did not speak for months. Contact, renewed by chance, restored nothing essential, and Sartre would later write of the period between 1946 and 1952 that 'we continued to see each other only by avoiding important subjects'.[65]

Neither Victims nor Executioners[66]

Beginning on 19 November 1946, Camus wrote a series of articles grouped under the title 'Neither Victims nor Executioners',[67] in which he expressed his refusal to choose between the violence of the colonizers and the counter-violence of the colonized, considering both equally reprehensible. This pacifist and moralizing position favours the status quo: it aims to preserve a situation in which the colonial order would no longer risk being threatened by popular insurrection. In his first article ('The Century of Fear'), Camus writes against political utopia but also against science: 'We are stifling among people who believe they are absolutely right, whether in their machines or in their ideas.'[68] For him, the only question that truly matters is how to escape certainties, which he conceives as a form of 'terror'. He advocates, first and foremost, a renunciation of all violence. One must therefore simultaneously refuse to be 'killed and brutalized' and to 'kill and brutalize'. Only in this way, according to Camus, can one escape what he sees as the pervasive terror of the twentieth century. In another

---

65 Jean-Paul Sartre, *Les Mots et autres écrits autobiographiques*, Paris: Gallimard, 2010, 949.

66 Some of what follows, including the description of Camus's series of articles can also be found in my *Albert Camus, A Very Short Introduction*, Oxford: Oxford University Press, 2020, 62–6.

67 Camus, *Œuvres complètes*, vol. II, 436–56. My translation.

68 Ibid., 437.

article, 'Mystified Socialism', Camus urges the Socialist Party to abandon revolution and Marxism as an absolute ideology. He promotes a relative utopia. He proposes a worldwide revolution – but without violence. In 'International Democracy and Dictatorship', he calls for an international democracy, which he distinguishes from the United Nations, viewed by him as a kind of dictatorship – although, according to his own logic, he specifies that resistance to the United Nations must not employ violent methods.

At the end of 1946, in a crucial passage from the article 'The World Is Moving Fast', Camus warns his readers of the imminence of a 'clash of civilizations': 'In ten years, in fifty years, it is the pre-eminence of Western civilization that will be in question.'[69] It is therefore necessary, he argues, to open the world parliament to 'these civilizations' (that is, non-European civilizations) in order to keep them within the colonial fold. These lines express the anxiety provoked by the questioning of the European's privileged status in the world – especially in the colonies.

The response in *Les Temps modernes* is scathing: 'Both Executioners and Victims'. The opening editorial notably compares the French army in Indochina to the Wehrmacht in France as an occupying force – a passage that provoked the ire of François Mauriac, who targeted Sartre in his capacity as editor of the journal. The editorial concludes with another attack, this time against those who defend French interventions through an 'opportunism' that barely conceals their 'deep connivance with overt or shamefaced colonialists'.[70] How can one fail to recognize Camus's position here?

Sartre would be even more explicit some twenty years later, in October 1965, during a lecture in Japan:

69　Ibid., 449.

70　'*Et boureaux et victomes*, in *Les Temps modernes*, December 1946, 1–2. The unsigned editorial was most likely written by Jean Pouillon.

For example, many false intellectuals at home said (about our war in Indochina or during the Algerian war): 'Our colonial methods are not what they ought to be; there are too many inequalities in our overseas territories. But I am opposed to all violence, wherever it comes from; I wish to be *neither executioner nor victim*, and that is why I oppose the uprising of the natives against the settlers.' It is clear to any mind that has radicalised itself that this pseudo-universalist stance amounts to declaring: 'I am in favour of the chronic violence that the colonists inflict on the colonized (over-exploitation, unemployment, malnourishment – maintained by terror); in any case it is the lesser evil and will eventually disappear of its own accord. But I oppose the violence that the colonised might employ in order to free themselves from the settlers who oppress them.'[71]

From the Sartrean perspective, violence is conceived as a motor of collective emancipation – a conception to which Camus is diametrically opposed. It is in opposition to this view that Camus elaborates his own theory of violence.

The Just Assassins: Codified Violence[72]

The rise to power of oppressed peoples was impossible to deny; even the future American president, John F. Kennedy – then a senator – would voice his concern a few years later on the floor of the Capitol: 'The worldwide struggle against imperialism, the sweep of nationalism, is the most potent force in foreign affairs today.'[73] Camus developed a theory of violence with the aim of retroactively (and all the more forcefully) validating his

71   Jean-Paul Sartre, *Playdoyer pour les intellectuels*, in *Situations VII*, Paris: Gallimard, 2001, 221–2. My translation and emphasis.

72   Some of what follows, including the summary of Camus's play, can also be found in my *Albert Camus, A Very Short Introduction*, 66–8.

73   Elaine Mokhtefi, *Algiers, Third World Capital*, London and New York: Verso, 2018, 31.

implicit condemnation of anti-colonial violence. He illustrated this theory through the play *The Just Assassins*[74] and a preliminary essay, 'The Delicate Murderers', published in January 1948 (an essay later incorporated, in a different form, into *The Rebel*). For violence to be justified in Camus's eyes, two conditions must be met: (a) the killer must participate directly in the act and, in doing so, (b) must be willing to risk his own life. Drawing on *Memoirs of a Terrorist* by Boris Savinkov, a former Russian 'terrorist' who attempted to assassinate the tsar in 1905, Camus staged the dilemma of political violence through a discussion among militants in a revolutionary cell advocating propaganda by deed and preparing the assassination of the tsar.

The three main characters are Ivan Kaliayev, Stepan Fedorov, and Dora Doulebov. At the outset, the characters are animated by what resembles an unshakeable faith in the legitimacy of their cause. Kaliayev, presented as the true hero, distinguishes himself by his scruples: he cannot throw the bomb because of the presence of the tsar's young nieces and nephews. On a second attempt, he succeeds in killing the grand duke, this time alone. Kaliayev is arrested and, although the authorities offer to pardon him if he betrays his comrades, he refuses. Executed by the state in the final act, Kaliayev is the hero of the play because his actions meet the very precise conditions prescribed by Camus that render violence acceptable: a willingness to risk one's life. Indeed, for Camus, one must die if one kills. This requirement serves as a guarantee that violence will not occur on a large scale, will be limited in time, and therefore will not lead to a 'tyrannical' regime.

Stepan, another member of the conspiratorial group, enthusiastically approves of the murder of innocents. He embodies a decidedly caricatural representation of the revolutionary militant: initially an advocate of collective punishment, he

---

74 Albert Camus, *Les Justes*, in *Œuvres complètes*, vol. III, Paris: Gallimard, 2008, 1–52.

quickly becomes a proponent of genocide. Stepan is violent, intolerant, and fanatical. In his view, the end justifies the means. To complete the picture, on a personal level he is fragile, petty, mean-spirited, and jealous; he ultimately admits that he envied Kaliayev. Dora, although a revolutionary militant, is ultimately shown to be motivated by her love for Kaliayev. After learning of his execution, she decides to continue the struggle, but only in order to be reunited with the man she loves in death. Throughout the play, the militants are more or less subtly assimilated to believers (a theme developed even further in *The Rebel*). Camus introduces an almost mystical dimension that ultimately transcends the revolutionary fervour of all the characters. The true generative force of the play is, in the end, Kaliayev's 'nobility', which inspires both Stepan's jealousy and Dora's devotion.

Camus contrasts Kaliayev's willingness to sacrifice himself with the posture he attributes to engaged intellectuals; for him, there are 'two races of men. One kills once and pays for it with his life. The other justifies thousands of crimes and accepts every kind of honour.'[75]

For Sartre, these concerns belonged to another age. In *Dirty Hands* (1948) – a play that also takes political violence as its subject, but from an entirely different perspective, that of seizing power rather than symbolic action – the central character, Hugo, hesitates, like Kaliayev, to kill for the cause; he is ridiculed by Louis, a hardline militant:

> **Hugo:** In Russia, at the end of the last century, there were guys who stood in the path of a grand duke with a bomb in their pocket. The bomb exploded, the grand duke was blown up and so was the guy.
>
> **Louis:** They were anarchists. You dream about them because you're like them: an anarchist intellectual. You are fifty years behind the times. Terrorism is over.

---

75 Camus, *L'Homme révolté*, in *Œuvres complètes*, vol. III, 209.

Hugo: Then I am useless.

Louis: In that respect, yes.[76]

This caricature of Camus's position sets the tone and foretells the break between the two men. Sartre here parodies what would become one of the central problematics of *The Rebel*.

The Rebel: Revolt against Revolution

In this essay, the absurd – whose nihilism sits uneasily in the postwar context – gives way to revolt, presented as a reaction, an individual corrective jolt against a vaguely defined injustice. Revolt is an emotion, a drive, rather than a thought; once again, as with the absurd, Camus does not explain but illustrates through examples and, above all, numerous counter-examples. *The Rebel* is meant to be to revolt what *The Myth of Sisyphus* was to the absurd: a blueprint.

The first example of revolt offered by the book is that of a slave who, after a lifetime of obedience, 'suddenly deems a new command unacceptable'.[77] Does his revolt lead to emancipation, or does it provoke repression by his masters? We never find out the answer: he exists only through his gesture and then disappears from the essay, unseen. This revolt prescribed by Camus is limited, individual, and fleeting.

The slave's appearance is brief, and one understands why. For Camus, the rebel will be European or will not be: 'The problem of revolt has meaning only within our own European societies.'[78] He adds that 'it is difficult for revolt to express itself in societies where inequalities are very great', or certain primitive societies where equality is 'absolute',[79] and concludes that

---

76 Jean-Paul Sartre, *Les Mains sales*, in *Théâtre complet, IIe tableau, scène IV*, p. 263. My translation.

77 Camus, *L'Homme révolté*, in *Œuvres complètes*, vol. III, 70.

78 Ibid., 77.

79 Ibid.

it also cannot occur in societies where the sacred occupies a central place. The reader might wonder about the French Revolution, which arose from a society almost entirely immersed in Catholicism. But Camus does not offer a sustained analysis here; rather, this commentary functions as a means of excluding colonized peoples from his discussion of revolt.

This vision of a Europe besieged by a primitive external world clearly echoes the idea of a coming 'clash of civilizations' that preoccupies him (already evoked in 'Neither Victims nor Executioners'). Composed at the height of anti-imperialist ferment, the text reveals itself as fundamentally reactionary.

But let us be clear: the central target of *The Rebel* is communism. As the text unfolds, the reviled ideology is renamed 'materialism', 'historical absolutism', 'absolute justice', or even 'German ideology'; whatever the label, it would inevitably lead humanity to 'terror', to 'historical murder', to 'perpetual injustice', and would constitute 'the total sum of evil'.[80] This is the leitmotif of the final section: 'Then, when revolution, in the name of power and history, becomes this murderous and excessive mechanism, a new revolt becomes sacred, in the name of measure and of life.'[81] If one must revolt, it must be against communism.

The argument opens with the following assertion: 'Absolute justice passes through the suppression of all contradiction; it destroys freedom.' Those who commit themselves to absolute justice – the communists – are distinguished from fascists in 'evil' by their 'historical vocation': 'we now know ... that revolution without limits other than historical effectiveness means servitude without limits'. For Camus, the remedy lies in a 'Mediterranean' or 'solar' thought that carries a troubling national dimension: 'The history of the First International, in which German socialism incessantly fights against the libertarian thought of the French, Spaniards, and Italians, is the history

80 Ibid., 306–22 *passim*.
81 Ibid., 322.

of the struggle between German ideology and the Mediterranean spirit.'[82] Ideas here are conflated with geographical origins, with nationalities. For Camus, Europe itself is divided into 'races':

> Cast into this ignoble Europe, where the proudest of races dies, stripped of all beauty and friendship, we Mediterraneans still live by the same light. At the heart of the European night, solar thought, the civilization with two faces, awaits its dawn.[83]

Towards what future? Camus spares us the answer.

Camus brandishes an undefined humanist morality – defined, if at all, by some rather troubling identity-based aspects – against any large-scale emancipatory project. The sole solution he advocates lies in a vague 'altruistic individualism'. Any disagreement with his viewpoint is treated as a voice in favour of organized murder and servitude. Revolt must, above all, not fundamentally call the social order into question.

Behind the façade of the moralist, Camus is writing *against*. His conviction that communism is inseparable from the emancipation of colonized peoples gives rise to a growing anxiety that becomes the driving force of his intellectual efforts. This fear motivates his hatred of the Hegelian notion of History and casts new light on the romanticism of his early work, his cult of nature, and the virulently anti-communist tone of *The Rebel*.

Criticism and Defence of *The Rebel*

Upon the publication of *The Rebel*, Francis Jeanson volunteered to write its review for *Les Temps modernes*. The two men held radically different conceptions of revolt. In 1951, Jeanson was particularly aware of the brutality of the French

---

82 Ibid., 317.
83 Ibid., 319.

colonial state in Algeria. He had visited Algeria in 1949, four years after the Sétif massacre, and wrote the following:

> And then I went to Sétif, where I was taken in hand by the deputy prefect. He showed me around his town. Standing in front of a mound of lime on a public square, he said, taking me familiarly by the arm: 'There, look – this is where it was.' He was speaking of the riots that took place on 8 May 1945. He went on proudly: 'You remember? They tried to get us, the Arabs! Well, we got them instead! A thousand for one, sir, a thousand for one!' It was lime – it was the bodies that had been burned, reduced to ashes ... For me, it was decisive: this man ... could not imagine that he might shock me by speaking this way! That day, my disgust turned into revolt.[84]

Jeanson later became a participant in the metropolitan struggle for Algerian independence alongside the FLN. Today, he is known above all for the eponymous network he organized, for which he was convicted of high treason by the courts.

Jeanson first notes that the book was well received by both the left and the right, and wonders whether this is not due to the fact that the work and its ideas are malleable, 'capable of taking on diverse forms'. Jeanson criticizes the Camusian panorama as a 'pseudo-history of revolutions'. Its theses? 'Pseudo-philosophy'.[85]

According to Jeanson, Camus's sole concern – indeed, his obsession – is Stalinism and its crimes. To neither mention nor take offence at the anti–working-class policies of the French government, or at the crimes committed by the French army in Madagascar and Indochina, is to make oneself their objective ally, Jeanson implies.

Camus sent a reply directly to Sartre. But he pretended no

---

84 Francis Jeanson, *Notre guerre*, Paris: Éditions de Minuit, 1955, 5. My translation.

85 Francis Jeanson, 'Albert Camus ou l'Âme révoltée', *Les Temps modernes*, no. 79 (1952): 2070–90.

longer to know him and addressed him as 'Monsieur le directeur des *Temps modernes*'.[86]

Beyond the form, the tone is stilted, extremely formal, almost tense. Camus refuses to discuss colonialism explicitly, except to claim for himself the title of former anti-colonialist fighter, with this ambiguous sentence: 'Those Algerians of whom [Jeanson] makes his daily bread were, until the war, my comrades in a rather uncomfortable struggle'[87] – a reference, left unexplained, to his support for the Blum–Viollette bill. Camus carefully cultivates confusion between anti-colonialism and the desire to reform colonialism. Having absolved himself, Camus issues an ultimatum: in order to continue this 'dialogue', he demands a clear condemnation of Soviet labour camps – despite the fact that they had already been unequivocally condemned by the *Les Temps modernes* team, and by Sartre himself.[88]

Sartre's response stands out for its style, erudition (references, whether in passing or at length, to Molière, Rembrandt, Mauriac, Breton, Gide, Chateaubriand, Bataille, Mallarmé, Rousseau, Baudelaire, Descartes, Pascal, and Hegel), but also for its corrosive humour: 'You have become the prey of a bleak *excess* that masks your inner difficulties and which you call, I believe, Mediterranean measure', followed by an uncompromising verdict: 'You hate the difficulties of thought and hastily decree that there is nothing to understand, in order to avoid the reproach of not having understood.'[89]

---

86   Albert Camus, 'Révolte et servitude', *Les Temps modernes*, no. 82 (1952), in *Œuvres complètes*, vol. III, 412–30.

87   Ibid., 421.

88   'Des jours de notre vie', ('Days of Our Lives'). *Les Temps modernes*, vol. 51, January 1950. In this editorial, Sartre and Merleau-Ponty denounce the labour camps in the USSR with great vehemence. 'One wonders what reasons remain for speaking of socialism in connection with the Soviet Union.' It should also be noted that six years later Sartre would condemn the Soviet intervention in Hungary and would break with the Party on that occasion.

89   Jean-Paul Sartre, 'Réponse à Albert Camus', *Les Temps*

Above all, Sartre moves beyond the binary opposition between Jeanson and Camus – the former proposing the condemnation of colonialism as a prerequisite, the latter that of the USSR – by synthesizing the two and exposing Camus's contradiction in the process: 'It often happens that the "slave" is the ally of one of those you call the masters ... If your principles are applied, the Vietnamese are colonised and therefore slaves; but they are communists and therefore tyrants.'[90] In Sartre's conclusion, his condemnation of the matter is clear: 'It seems to me ... that the only way to help the slaves over there [the colonized] is to take the side of those over here [the working class in France]'.[91] Sartre also takes aim at Camus's political archaism by referring to a crucial scene in *The Plague* in which the narrator, Dr Rieux, asks Father Paneloux how one can still believe in God when He allows children to die of the plague. Sartre has no use for this bourgeois humanism, still frozen in the eighteenth century, with its debates rich in pathos but obsolete. They have the dubious merit of privileging metaphysical questions at the expense of social ones:

> A child was dying; you accused the absurdity of the world and that deaf and blind God you had created so that you could spit in his face; but the child's father, if he was unemployed or a worker, accused society: he knew full well that the absurdity of our condition is not the same in Passy [a bourgeois neighbourhood] as it is in Billancourt [a working-class one].[92]

As a distant echo of his earlier 'Explanation of *The Stranger*', Sartre also offers Camus a brief lesson on freedom: it is 'nothing other than our free choice to fight in order to become free'.[93]

---

modernes, no. 82 (1952). Reprinted in *Situations IV*, Paris: Gallimard, 1993, 91.
90 Ibid., 107.
91 Ibid., 107.
92 Ibid., 118.
93 Ibid., 110.

Following this public exchange, Sartre was widely regarded as having prevailed over Camus, who, depressed and furious, briefly contemplated coming to blows. He avoided the Latin Quarter and the cafés frequented by Sartre and Beauvoir and went to the countryside as often as possible. He wrote a long, detailed response to all the criticisms, entitled 'Defence of *The Rebel*', which would be published only posthumously.[94]

A few months after the break, something strange occurred: Camus appeared to reverse himself on a crucial issue and to change his position radically. Less than a year after the publication of *The Rebel*, in a preface to *Moscow under Lenin* by Alfred Rosmer – a veteran communist who had lived in Russia from 1921 to 1924 and who knew and admired Lenin and Trotsky – Camus wrote that the Soviet Revolution marked the beginning of something new, a new hope, and that Stalin's crimes should never lead one to reject the ideal and hope of communism. To say the least, this does not align with the central thesis of *The Rebel*, which condemns the very idea of communism as axiomatically leading to servitude.

Camus adopted the same position again at a rally in Saint-Étienne, declaring that the Russian Revolution of 1917 was a positive moment in history. What emerges is an impression of confusion between the radically anti-communist stance of *The Rebel*, his friendly preface to the book of a revolutionary syndicalist sympathetic to Bolshevism, and his speeches before working-class audiences. This contradiction can likely be explained by the fact that his anti-communism only manifested itself once communists and communist sympathizers integrated the struggle against capitalism with the struggle against colonialism. Perhaps he thought he had gone too far in *The Rebel*, or perhaps he adjusted his viewpoint too readily to his interlocutors – or perhaps he was indeed 'capable of taking on diverse forms', to use Jeanson's words. Be that as it may, it

---

94 Camus, *Œuvres complètes*, vol. III, 366–78.

is important to note this belated praise of the Russian Revolution by the man who had become – well before 1989 – the standard-bearer of the French, if not global, anti-communist intelligentsia. Contemporary readings according to which Sartre favoured tyranny while Camus defended freedom are structured around the former's anti-colonial engagement and the latter's anti-communism, rather than on an objective assessment of their respective trajectories and commitments.

Today, Camus and Sartre have become paradoxically inseparable: they represent antithetical positions in the fundamental debates on racism and social oppression in all its forms. The popularity of one corresponds to the unpopularity of the other, and in a France that, as the historian Malika Rahal puts it, has 'never made its anticolonial turn',[95] it is easier to understand why Camus is fashionable.

---

95 Interview with Rachida El Azzouzi, *Mediapart*, 25 June 2022.

4

The Anti-Sartre

In Algeria, a single electoral college, if there are as many voters among Arabs as among Europeans, is impossible. One cannot place on the same footing a population that is mature and another that lacks maturity. Democracy consists in an equality that is not numerical. That is what I said in a confidential report I was asked to write for an advisory group in a position to influence government decisions.

– Albert Camus[1]

The Fall

Have you read *Monsieur de Bougrelon*,[2] Jean Lorrain's great critical success originally published in 1897? It is a novel set in Amsterdam in which the eponymous narrator, a Frenchman in voluntary exile, meets another Parisian expatriate (not very talkative) at the Manchester Café and tells him numerous anecdotes.

Have you read Albert Camus's *The Fall* (1956)? The action takes place in a bar – Mexico City – located in the same Amsterdam neighbourhood as the Manchester. A character named Jean-Baptiste Clamence (very talkative) recounts his

---

1 Albert Camus, quoted in Jean Grenier, *Carnets 1944–1971*, Paris: Seghers, 1991, 224.

2 Jean Lorrain, *Monsieur de Bougrelon*, Paris: Henri Jonquières, 1928. In English, cf. *Monsieur de Bougrelon and Other Stories*, Snuggly Books, 2020.

life to an anonymous Parisian stranger, who listens a great deal and speaks little.

Léon-François Hoffmann compiled the similarities between the two books at the conclusion of his article 'A Source for *The Fall*: *Monsieur de Bougrelon*': 'Parallels, then, in the setting, in the novelistic duration, in the plotline, in the characters, in the behaviours, in the metaphorical structure – these cannot be accidental resemblances.'[3] That said, rather than plagiarism, what we have here is an homage: the similarities exist, but the stories differ.

Camus shared at least one further trait with Lorrain, who, likewise, led a tumultuous social life – though one that was far more dangerous. A controversial figure of decadence, he delighted in provoking his contemporaries: at the time, disputes were often settled by duels (Jean Lorrain fought, among others, Marcel Proust). It is precisely in these terms that M. de Bougrelon explains his presence in Amsterdam: he is forced into exile following a duel. After the break with Sartre, an irritated Camus expressed in his *Notebooks* a certain nostalgia for that era:

> A noble profession in which one must allow oneself to be insulted without flinching by a literary or party lackey! In other times, said to be degrading, one at least retained the right to issue a challenge without ridicule – and to kill. Idiotic, of course, but it made insult less comfortable.[4]

Far from the heroism of a duel, we must content ourselves in *The Fall* with a banal altercation – an anecdote central to the narrative – between a motorcyclist and a driver, which turns into a public humiliation for Clamence, the narrator; a humiliation he 'took a long time to forget'. Driving in Paris, Clamence is insulted in full view of everyone by the motorcyclist, 'a dry

---

3   Léon-François Hoffmann, 'Une source de *La Chute* : *Monsieur de Bougrelon*', *Revue d'histoire littéraire de la France*, no. 1 (1969): 93–100. My translation.

4   Camus, *Œuvres complètes*, vol. IV, 1179.

little man, wearing a monocle and golf pants'. He lunges to strike him, but, instead, a third party (whom he bitterly nick-names 'd'Artagnan') lands a punch on his head, and he has to leave, crestfallen: 'I had, in short, publicly wimped out.' The memory of the incident haunts him: 'I ran that little film through my imagination a hundred times.'[5] It is the rumination of a revenge:

> I pictured myself flooring d'Artagnan with a good hook, getting back into my car, chasing the cretin [the motorcyclist] who had hit me, catching up with him, pinning his machine against the curb, dragging him aside, and giving him the beating he richly deserved.[6]

After his public humiliation in *Les Temps modernes*, Camus had wanted to administer a beating to Sartre but thought better of it because, he claimed, Sartre was too small.[7]

The Fall examines the frantic resentment felt by a man who believes himself to be attacked on all sides and who, like Camus after Jeanson's and Sartre's takedowns of *The Rebel*, cannot overcome a violent desire for revenge.

After the nearly ritual precautions affirming the autonomy of the work of art from private life – emphasizing that Cla-mence is neither Sartre nor Camus – almost all commentators, from Cruise O'Brien to Todd, converge in siding with Charles Augustin Sainte-Beuve against Proust: *The Fall* was, after all, a biographical narrative, making its protagonist at times an alter ego of Sartre and, at times, of Camus himself.

---

5   Camus, *La Chute*, in *Œuvres complètes*, vol. III, 719.

6   Ibid., 719–20.

7   In a letter to his pied-noir friend Robert Jaussaud (in Patrick McCarthy, *Camus: A Critical Study of His Life and Work*, London: Hamish Hamilton, 1982, 259), he laments that their 'Algerian' methods for settling such matters were considered unacceptable in Paris. He also mentions Sartre's short stature as an obstacle to resolving problems in this way, in a conversation with Jeanne Terracini (see Olivier Todd, *Albert Camus, une vie*, Paris: Gallimard, 1999, 790).

Let us suppose two Clamences in *The Fall*, one representing Sartre, the other Camus. We would then have to separate the 'judge' from the 'penitent'.[8] The first 'profits' from the misfortunes of the oppressed; he is the humanist good conscience that preaches freedom (which leads, according to Camus, to 'servitude'); he is a proud 'judge' (though a lawyer by trade), haloed by his status as saviour. We are, of course, meant to recognize Sartre:

> I had a specialty: noble causes. The widow and the orphan, as people say – I don't know why, since after all there are abusive widows and ferocious orphans. It was enough, however, for me to sniff on a defendant the slightest odor of victimhood for my sleeves to swing into action. And what action! A tempest! My heart was on my sleeves. You'd have thought justice slept with me every night.[9]

Yet his good deeds are only vanity: justice and freedom are devalued by his posturing. His whole persona is identified with double-talk. Another confession by Clamence seems to mimic the Sartrean conception of freedom:

> Once upon a time, I was always talking of freedom. At breakfast I used to spread it on my toast, I used to chew it all day long, and in company my breath was delightfully redolent of freedom.[10]

This judge is a coward who pretends to believe in justice and freedom, but whose actions scarcely correspond to his speeches. The entire narrative is strewn with jabs that function as so many references to their public epistolary exchange.

---

8   The word penitent caricatures Sartre's struggles – against the interests of his own social class and against the colonial interests of his country – as though they were acts of repentance; these commitments would amount to nothing more than class guilt and bourgeois self-hate – this facile psychologism reading runs through Camus's work after their break.

9   Camus, *Œuvres complètes*, vol. III, 703–4.

10   Ibid., 707.

Here another Clamence overlays the first: one who repents, becoming the 'penitent' who regrets his past actions. His boasts become confessions: one November night, he let a woman drown in the Seine.

> On the bridge … I made out a slim young woman dressed in black … I went on my way … when I heard the sound … tremendous in the nocturnal silence – of a body striking the water … I wanted to run and I did not move … I felt an irresistible weakness invade my body. I have forgotten what I thought then. 'Too late, too far…' or something of the sort. I was still listening, motionless. Then, with small steps, in the rain, I walked away. I warned no one.[11]

This episode haunts him, and years later, on a boat trip, he sees 'a large black spot' that he takes for a person drowning in the ocean.

> I was going to shout, to call stupidly for help, when I saw it again. It was one of those bits of debris ships leave behind them … I understood then … that the cry that had sounded on the Seine behind me, years earlier, had not ceased … I understood too that it would go on waiting for me on the seas and rivers – everywhere, in the end.[12]

This Clamence *after* the confession is indeed Camus. He is the anti-Sartre.

These two egos, coexisting and opposing one another, must be conceived as parts of a single whole; for Clamence, his past errors and his present repentance join in a definitive synthesis: there is no justice, there is no hope.

This is the dialectic of *The Fall*: the judge who defends 'widows and orphans' for selfish reasons but lets the woman who throws herself into the Seine die, is opposed to the penitent

---

11 Ibid., 728.
12 Ibid., 765.

who, full of regret, utters this plea: 'Oh young girl, throw yourself into the water again so that I may have, a second time, the chance to save us both!'[13] How long does penitence last? The duration of the narrative *and* the instant of its final sentence:

> A second time, eh – what imprudence! Suppose … they took us at our word? We'd have to go through with it. Brr … the water is so cold! But let us reassure ourselves! It is too late now; it will always be too late. Fortunately![14]

In a double negative, Camus denigrates commitment as well as repentance – everything is stage-managed. We are left in an anomic world without values, where no genuine participation is possible. This is finally a textbook illustration of *mauvaise foi* and the impossibility of *sincérité*. (But why then does Camus not get credit for this performance? Why even for the benevolent readers is it more damaging for Camus himself than for Sartre, who it wants to denounce?)

This mechanism of renunciation has its antagonist: Sartre's 'Black Orpheus dialectic', in his famous preface to the poetic anthology edited by Léopold Sédar Senghor (1947). Strongly inspired by Aimé Césaire's play *And the Dogs Were Silent* (1943), Sartre opposes colonial racism to the colonized subject, who is oppressed 'in his race and because of it'. It is, therefore, first and foremost 'of his race that he must become conscious'. Sartre conceives this awakening (in this case, *négritude*) as a stage towards a final unity 'that will bring all the oppressed closer together'. The colonized subject,

> because he has suffered more than anyone else from capitalist oppression … demands the abolition of ethnic privileges wherever they come from; he affirms his solidarity with the oppressed of every color. As a result, the subjective, existential,

---

13 Ibid., 765.
14 Ibid.

ethnic notion of *négritude* 'passes', as Hegel would say, into that – objective, positive, exact – notion of the proletariat.[15]

'You're going too fast!', Fanon replies, in substance, in *Black Skin, White Masks* (1952):

> Against historical becoming, there was unpredictability to be set in opposition. I needed to lose myself completely in *negritude*. One day, perhaps, in the depths of that unhappy romanticism ...[16]

This critique profoundly influenced Sartre, who set aside his synthesis in order to focus, instead, on the second movement of the dialectic: anti-colonial counter-violence, which he theorized in *Critique of Dialectical Reason* and forcefully endorsed in his controversial preface to *The Wretched of the Earth* (1961). In the latter, Fanon ultimately returns to the Sartrean synthesis he had initially criticized – for example, in the conclusion of the chapter entitled 'On National Culture':

> The most urgent task for the African intellectual is the construction of his nation. If this construction is genuine – that is to say, if it expresses the manifest will of the people, if it reveals in their impatience the African peoples – then national construction necessarily entails the discovery and promotion of universalising values. Far from distancing the nation from others, national liberation is what brings the nation onto the stage of history. It is at the very heart of national consciousness that international consciousness arises and comes to life.[17]

---

15   Jean-Paul Sartre, *Orphée noir*, *Situations III, littérature et engagement*, Paris: Gallimard, 2013, 301.

16   Frantz Fanon, *Peau noire, masques blancs*, Paris: Le Seuil, 1971, 109.

17   Frantz Fanon, *Les Damnés de la terre (The Wretched of the Earth)*, Paris: La Découverte, 2006, 235.

Fanon and Sartre engage in dialogue: they oppose one another and then reunite within a utopian, universalist, and anti-racist project.

We are at the opposite extreme of the nihilistic dialectic of *The Fall*,[18] where, in the end, everything is equivalent: oppression and liberation merge within Camus's lexical field; 'slavery' becomes synonymous with 'servitude', which, in turn, becomes synonymous with 'communism'.

Let us now reconsider the central scene of *The Fall*: Clamence abandons the unknown woman to her fate and refuses to become involved. Above all, he does not want to know what happens to her: 'Neither the next day nor the days that followed did I read the newspapers.'[19] This refusal to become involved mirrors Camus's own decision to stop writing about Algeria in the midst of the War of Independence – his famous 'silence', his refusal of public debate.

The Fall marks a return of sorts to the nihilistic absurd of Camus's early texts: Clamence is a sophisticated Meursault who had gone on to complete his studies. In *The Ethics of Ambiguity* (1947), Simone de Beauvoir draws a distinction between existentialism and the absurd: 'One must not confuse the notion of ambiguity with that of absurdity. To declare existence absurd is to deny that it can give itself meaning; to say that it is ambiguous is to posit that meaning is never fixed, that it must constantly be won.'[20] She conceived this text as a defence of existential political engagement:

> Just as one must not lightly give in to impulses of pity or generosity, neither must one stubbornly serve an abstract morality;

---

18 Monsieur de Bougrelon – let us return to him for a moment – dying at the end of the novel, is compared to 'a statue of Orpheus, a macabre Orpheus': Lorrain, *Monsieur de Bougrelon*, 169.

19 Camus, *La Chute*, in *Œuvres complètes*, vol. III, 729.

20 Simone de Beauvoir, *Pour une morale de l'ambiguïté*, Paris: Gallimard, 2017, p. 170. My translation.

violence is justified only if it offers concrete possibilities to the freedom I claim to be saving; in exercising it, I willingly or unwillingly take on a commitment towards others and towards myself; a man whom I wrest from death he had chosen has the right to come and ask me for the means and the reasons to live; tyranny exercised against a sick person can be justified only by his recovery; whatever the purity of the intention that animates me, every unilateral exercise of power is a fault for which I must seek forgiveness. Nor am I in a position to make such decisions with regard to just anyone: *the example of the stranger who throws himself into the Seine and about whose rescue I hesitate, is entirely abstract; in the absence of any concrete connection with this despairing person, my choice can never be anything more than sheer facticity.*[21]

Unsurprisingly, Camus read *The Ethics of Ambiguity* (initially published in the November and December 1946 issues of *Les Temps modernes*) with a certain displeasure. Beauvoir recounts his reaction in 1946:

He made a few caustic remarks to me; in his eyes I was sinning against 'French clarity'. We, for our part, felt that in the name of this ideal he often settled for a limited intellectual framework – not out of frivolity, but by deliberate choice: he was protecting himself.[22]

In *The Fall*, all the ambiguities posed and articulated by Beauvoir are swept aside. There is an unrecognized Don Quixote in Clamence – and in Camus as well, minus the irony. All of this leads to nihilism – but a nihilism that does not acknowledge itself and is experienced as a sin.

Sartre also questioned the central dilemma of *The Fall* by way of parody in the opening of his play *Nekrassov* (1955).

---

21   Ibid., 169–70. My emphasis.
22   Simone de Beauvoir, *La Force des choses*, in *Mémoires*, vol. I, Paris: Gallimard, 2018, 1048–9.

Had Sartre heard about Camus's project, or had they discussed it beforehand? Both hypotheses are plausible. So, too, is the idea of Camus's work being a response to Sartre's play.

In the first scene, on the banks of the Seine in Paris, near a bridge, a homeless couple, Irma and Robert, see a man, Georges, throw himself into the river. The couple argue throughout the entire scene: should they save him or not? Tragedy is turned into farce. After much hesitation, the homeless man, Robert, finally throws a rope to the man, who grabs it:

> **Irma:** … He hauls himself on his own. Saved! Aren't you proud of yourself? I feel proud. It's as if you'd given me a child.
> **Robert:** You see! There are not only bad people in life. If I'd met someone like me to pull me out of the gutter…
> (Georges appears, the water running from him.)
> **Georges** (furious): You bloody fools…
> **Irma** (sadly): There you are!
> **Robert:** That's human ingratitude for you!
> **Georges** (taking hold of the homeless man and shaking him): *What are you sticking your nose in for, you lousy parasite? Who do you think you are – Providence?*[23]

Exile and the Kingdom

Camus's writings, up to *The First Man*, tend to conceal both his impossible hope for a humane colonialism and his profound fear of anything that might resemble, even remotely, an independent Algeria. Camus's writing – often vague and indeterminate, one of the reasons for its success – is not a stylistic effect: it is the expression of a man haunted by thoughts he knows to be unsayable.

In the short-story collection *Exile and the Kingdom* (1957), the last work of fiction published during his lifetime, the veneer

---

23 Jean-Paul Sartre, *Nekrassov*, in *Théâtre complet*, Paris: Gallimard, 2005, 700. My translation and emphasis.

cracks. One year after the book appeared, Camus would publicly state what he really thought: 'As far as Algeria is concerned, national independence is a purely emotional response to the situation.'[24]

In these six stories, three registers dominate: anger, paternalism, and resentment. The anger of the European in Algeria, who lived within an everyday racism he did not question, is directed at the committed intellectual who supports independence. Beneath the cover of a parable, Camus's personal resentment towards Sartre and his crude anti-communism are here brought together in an extreme form. In 'The Renegade',[25] the intellectual appears in barely disguised fashion in the figure of a failed missionary, converted by those he had sought to convert: a population living in the vicinity of the former salt mines of Taghaza (Niger). The missionary is taken prisoner and tortured. The text, in the form of a long interior monologue, unfolds the thoughts and sufferings of this man whose tongue is torn out and whose mouth is finally filled with salt. The entire story is nothing but moral uncertainty and detailed physical suffering (the groans of the mutilated man – 'râ', 'râ' – punctuate the narrative). Shocked by the violence of the text, Camus's mentor, Jean Grenier, asked him what this story, 'in which a young missionary is tortured by savages and ends up converting to the religion of his torturers', could possibly mean. Camus replied: 'In this parable, it is the intellectual who has become a communist – the intellectual who ends by worshipping the religion of evil.'[26] This religion is, of course, communism, assimilated to the religion of the populations the missionary had sought to convert. It is here that Camus's visceral anti-communism and aversion to African cultures and religions converge; the two

---

24 Albert Camus, 'Algérie 1958', in *Œuvres complètes*, vol. IV, 388.

25 Albert Camus, *Le Renégat*, in *L'Exil et le Royaume*, *Œuvres complètes*, vol. IV, 19–33.

26 Jean Grenier, *Carnets, 1944–1971*, Paris: Seghers, 1991, 197.

categories – treated as equivalent – merge in his mind into a single 'religion of evil'.

Anger turns into contempt, into insults directed at Algerians and voiced by the husband in 'The Adulterous Woman'.[27] A pied-noir shopkeeper, Marcel, takes his wife, Janine, into the Algerian interior to purchase goods and sell them. Throughout the story, Janine experiences the presence of Algerians as oppressive and despises their 'stupid arrogance'. Marcel agrees: 'They think they can get away with anything now.' Other passages, present only in the confidential edition of the story published in 1954 (just 300 copies) and even more explicit, were removed by Camus for the edition intended for the general public. While waiting for his coffee, which is slow to arrive, Marcel grows impatient: ' "We want them to evolve," says Marcel. "To evolve, you have to work. And for them, work is like pork – forbidden." ' Of Algerians in general: 'They're all the same.' Camus's first editor, Roger Quilliot, speculates: 'One may wonder whether, in removing these [phrases], Camus did not wish, given the Algerian War, to soften the spontaneously racist character of Marcel's reactions.'[28] It now mattered to him to present a less brutal image of the settlers.

The story, nonetheless, offers a way of escaping these Algerians who so trouble the colonists: while Marcel remains alone with his anger and resentment, Janine finds an antidote in nature. Janine betrays her husband with the night, the stars, the Algerian desert. This quasi-mystical communion produces the liberating effect – at least for her – of silencing the noises of the Arab city. That moment of communion with nature, which had constituted Camus's happiness in the era of 'Nuptials at Tipasa' – the celebration of paid vacations inaugurated in 1936 – has been transformed into an (unnameable) colonial fantasy: an Algeria without Algerians.

---

27 Camus, 'La Femme adultère', in *Œuvres complètes*, vol. IV, 2–19.

28 Camus, *Théâtre, récits, nouvelles*, 2042, n. 3. My translation.

In 'The Guest', paternalism alternates with resentment. The protagonist, Daru, a pied-noir schoolteacher, lives in a house in the Algerian mountains that also serves as a primary school. One winter day, a man named Balducci, a policeman, arrives on a donkey, dragging at the end of a rope an Algerian man accused of having killed a member of his family. As in *The Stranger*, the man has no name. Daru is requisitioned: he is to escort the man to the authorities, something he is reluctant to do. But Balducci makes this a matter of loyalty and honour, insisting that Daru take the Algerian to prison. Although Daru accepts without question Balducci's account of events and the Algerian man's guilt, he does not want to hand him over. At the same time, he does not want to anger Balducci. To heighten the pressure further, Balducci announces that a conflict is imminent: 'If they rise up, no one will be safe; we're all in the same boat.'[29]

It is clear: even though Daru does not want to play any role in the affair, events are catching up with him. In the end, he agrees to sign a receipt confirming the prisoner's presence but refuses to promise to deliver him. Once Balducci has left, Daru feels guilty.

He is indeed caught between his anger towards the Algerian, whom he believes to be guilty, and towards Balducci, for having put him in this position. He takes the man to a place halfway between the town and the nomads. The choice is simple: go to the town, to the prison, or go south, to the Bedouins. Daru leaves him free to decide. Inexplicably, after hesitating for a time, the Arab heads towards the town. And Daru returns home. Camus portrays Daru as a man caught between two factions, a good man trying to be fair. Everything is arranged so that the reader feels empathy for Daru and his dilemma, which heightens the staging of the final paragraph: back in his classroom, Daru sees written in chalk on the blackboard the

---

29   Camus, 'L'Hôte', in *Œuvres complètes*, vol. IV, 51.

following message: 'You handed over our brother. You will pay.' The final, pathos-laden sentence describes Daru's state of mind: 'In this country he had loved so much, he was alone.'[30]

Good, just, alone, under pressure from his own people, threatened by Algerians, misunderstood by *everyone* – this is how Camus saw himself, or how he wanted to be seen, in the midst of the War of Independence. Note that this story presents the colonist as victim, as educator, as saviour; in this eminently paternalistic portrait one can also perceive resentment: the colonist is depicted as the misunderstood victim of ungrateful and violent natives.

This propagandistic aspect would be amplified to such an extent in *The First Man* that, after Camus's death in January 1960, those closest to him deemed it prudent to postpone its publication to a more favourable time. Ultimately it was not to be published until 1994.

The First Man: A Settler Named Adam

If, as Sartre writes in *Critique of Dialectical Reason*, the automatic negation of the colonized person's human identity is constitutive of the colonizers' identity, then one may argue that the anonymity imposed on Algerians in *The Stranger* and *The Plague* provides an instance of this mechanism; in his work, Camus reproduces the serial unity of the colonizer. This unity is founded on a vision of the colonized – here, the 'Arab' – as the 'absolute Other'. It is reinforced and sustained by the fact that, within this imaginary, the Arab represents a permanent threat to the colonial collective.

The subaltern status of Algerians in *The Stranger* and *The Plague* is neither explained nor discussed nor questioned; on the contrary, it is presented as an unquestionable given. This

---

30 Ibid., 58.

once again corresponds to Sartre's conception of racism in the *Critique*: '*It is not a thought at all*. It cannot even be formulated ... In reality, racism is the colonial interest lived as a link of all the colonialists of the colony through the serial flight of alterity.'[31] Yet, years later, in the midst of the Algerian War of Independence – a period during which denial was almost impossible – Camus attempted precisely to explain settler racism in *The First Man*. This novel, with strong autobiographical overtones, tells the story of Jacques Cormery, born in Algeria and living in France, who returns to his country of birth to reawaken memories of his deceased father.

Set during the war, the narrative alternates between dialogues involving settlers and Cormery and the latter's childhood memories. Cormery is confronted with the anger of the pieds-noirs in the face of the rise of Algerian nationalism. These exchanges make up the bulk of the text; they often stage an intransigent settler alongside another who is more understanding.

An emblematic dialogue illustrating this mechanism recalls a quarrel between an M. Levesque and his friend, Cormery's father – a soldier in the French army – that took place during the Rif War. The point of contention is the humanity of the 'Other':

> At the foot of a hedge of prickly pears, they found their comrade with his head back, bizarrely facing toward the moon. And at first they did not recognize his head because of its strange shape. But it was very simple. His throat had been cut and that ghastly swelling in his mouth was his entire penis. That was when they saw the body, with the legs spread wide, the Zouave's trousers slashed, and, in the middle of the gap, that swampy puddle, which they could see by the now indirect light of the moon. A hundred meters farther on, this time behind a large rock, the second sentinel was displayed in the same position ... At dawn,

---

31 Jean-Paul Sartre, *Critique of Dialectical Reason*, New York: Verso, 2004, 300 n88. My emphasis.

when they had gone back up to camp, Cormery [sr.] said their enemies were not men. Levesque, who was thinking about it, answered that for them that was how men should act, that we were in their own country, that they fought by all means necessary.

Cormery's face had taken on a stubborn look. 'Maybe. But they're wrong. A man doesn't do that.'

Levesque said that according to the other side, there were certain circumstances in which a man was supposed to do anything and [destroy everything].

But Cormery had shouted as if crazed with anger: 'No, a man doesn't let himself do that kind of thing! That's what makes a man, or otherwise …'. Then, he calmed down. 'As for me', he said in a low voice, 'I'm poor, I came from an orphanage, they put me in this uniform, they dragged me into the war, but I wouldn't let myself do that.'

'There are Frenchmen who do it,' [said] Levesque.

'Then they too, they aren't men.' And suddenly he cried out: 'A *filthy race! What a race! All of them, all* …'.[32]

It should be noted that, in most of the dialogues that run through the work, one of the settlers calls into question the humanity of the colonized. It should also be noted that the atrocities attributed to Moroccans are described in detail, whereas the crimes of Europeans are mentioned only briefly. The passage closes with an unequivocal judgement voiced by the paternal figure – otherwise constantly praised throughout the novel: the reader is left with this essentialist outcry ('dirty race'), presented as the understandable reaction of a traumatized victim.

Another attempt at explanation follows, this time concerning what the narrator calls the xenophobia of the pieds-noirs:

---

32 Albert Camus, *Le Premier homme*, in *Œuvres complètes*, vol. IV, 66–7. My emphasis.

> Unemployment, against which there was no protection, was the most dreaded evil [among the settlers]. This explained why these workers – whether in Peter's case or in Paul's – who in everyday life were always the most tolerant of men, were invariably xenophobic when it came to matters of work, successively accusing Italians, Spaniards, Jews, Arabs, and ultimately the whole world of stealing their jobs – an attitude certainly bewildering to intellectuals who theorize about the proletariat, yet nonetheless deeply human and readily excusable.[33]

The xenophobic attitude of French workers living in Algeria, and the fact that their primary identity is defined by race or nationality, is not questioned or criticized but is, in fact, validated in the novel. The social configuration – that is, the organization into social classes – is described as subordinate to national and religious identities; this subordination is not identified as problematic but, on the contrary, is defended as excusable because it is 'human'. This attempt to justify xenophobia points to a conception of humanity as driven by purely identitarian atavisms. What emerges is an essentialist vision of the world that is clearly far removed from existentialism, and one can retrospectively understand Camus's persistent refusal to allow himself to be defined as such.

The principal adversary in this pro-colonial line of argument, which recurs in *The First Man*, is not the Algerian but the anti-colonial metropolitan left fighting for Algerian independence, one of whose leading figures is none other than Jean-Paul Sartre, one of those 'intellectuals who theorize about the proletariat'.[34]

A typical victim of these supposed traitors to the colonial fatherland is a pied-noir winegrower who spends three days tearing up the vines on his property so that the 'Arabs' will not benefit from them. 'Young man, since what we have done

---

33   Ibid., 237.
34   Ibid., 236.

is a crime, it must be erased,' he says bitterly to Cormery. The landowner is portrayed as a tragic figure: an admirable man, a stoic and moving victim, an old settler from among 'those who are insulted in Paris'.[35] Yet this destruction of the vineyards echoes the darkest hours of the conquest of Algeria. In 1840, Tocqueville's friend General de Lamoricière and the future governor of Algeria, Bugeaud, agreed to implement the practice of the *razzia*: the destruction of villages, the killing of all the men who lived there (as well as the sale of the surviving women), and the theft of livestock. The directive was clear: it was necessary to 'prevent the Arabs from deriving any use of their land'.[36] The destruction of arable land and the uprooting of olive trees marked the true beginning of France's lasting occupation of Algeria. Nearly ninety years later, faced with the prospect of having to share these expropriated lands, Europeans in Algeria once again destroyed Algerian land – but, this time, Camus presents them to readers as victims suffering an injustice.

This indulgent portrayal of settlers' grievances functions as a refrain throughout the novel. Their resentment towards the metropole is illustrated by a conversation between Camus's alter ego (Cormery) and a farmer who tells him: 'I sent my family to Algiers and I'll die here [in the Algerian countryside]. They don't understand that in Paris.'[37] This resentment, this hatred, is virulent: since the very humanity of metropolitan French people is contested, the winegrower advises 'his' Algerian workers to join the FLN *maquis*, because 'there are no men left in France'. Here we find, in addition to machismo, the paternalism of pied-noir landowners who, even in defeat, presume to show Algerian agricultural workers the way forward.

---

35   Ibid., 167.

36   Charles-André Julien, *Histoire de l'Algérie contemporaine (1827–1871)*, vol. I, Paris: Presses Universitaires de France, 1964, 177–91. My translation.

37   Camus, *Le Premier homme*, 167.

This obsession with metropolitan pro-independence activists, perceived as a fifth column, is another way of minimizing the role of Algerians in their own liberation. Yet this proves impossible: the 'Arabs' are omnipresent throughout the text.

It is here that one realizes that the driving force of the narrative – without this ever being explicitly stated by the narrator – is the Algerian people and the fear they inspire. The entire text illustrates a reworking of the master/slave dialectic developed by Fanon: the settler takes the colonized into account only because of violence, or the threat of violence. It is at this price that the latter is recognized as a human being as such in the world – and in Camus's fiction. Even though, as usual in Camus's writings, settlers are labelled 'Algerians' and Algerians 'Arabs',[38] the latter are at the heart of the text. Once again, the author inadvertently offers an illustration of the very theses he rejected with all his strength throughout his life.

This fear of Algerians generates a haunting obsession. Nearly 300 years earlier, Spinoza had recounted a disturbing dream he had about black slaves in the service of the Netherlands:

> The images that had presented themselves to me during my sleep appeared before my eyes with as much vividness as if they had been real objects, in particular that of a black and filthy Brazilian whom I had never seen before. This image would largely disappear when, in order to distract myself with another object, I fixed my eyes on a book or something else; but as soon as I turned away from it and no longer fixed my gaze attentively on anything, the same image of the same Ethiopian reappeared before me with the same vividness, repeatedly, until gradually it faded away.[39]

---

38 For Camus, indeed, an 'Algerian' is of European origin and Christian: 'For them, as for most Algerians, religion was part of their civic life and that alone. They were Catholic as they were French; it entailed a certain number of rituals': ibid., 165.

39 Baruch Spinoza, Letter to Pieter Balling, in *Œuvres complètes*, Paris: Gallimard, 1955, 1116. My translation.

It is often through dreams that an (involuntary) awareness of exploited peoples makes itself felt. For Cormery, the nightmare is the unconscious admission of a worldview organized around ethnic, national, and chromatic divisions, which render aspirations to independence a mortal threat to Europeans. The dream of Cormery, the hero of *The First Man*, which can be found in the preparatory notes for the novel in the French editions, anticipates the essentialist fantasy that conceives of the sovereignty of colonized peoples only as the future enslavement of Europe:

> He dreams it during his afternoon nap. Tomorrow, six hundred million Yellows, billions of Yellows, of Blacks, of dark-skinned peoples, would sweep over the shores of Europe ... and at best convert it. Then everything that had been taught to him and to those who looked like him, everything he himself had learned – from that day on the men of his race, all the values for which he had lived – would die of uselessness.[40]

The antidote to this inevitable reversal is twofold: the prose first turns to a colonial nostalgia that is, all in all, fairly conventional, but also obsolete and ineffective, before ultimately intensifying and revealing itself as a hymn of veneration to nature; this movement grows stronger over the course of the novel.

First, nostalgia: this quasi-autobiographical novel, in which several temporal layers overlap (the past, childhood set against the present, civil war, adulthood, and the future), is a collection of memories repeatedly interrupted by events contemporaneous with the writing of the text. It is also a paean to a time when Algerians did not rebel with the intensity of the 1950s, a nostalgia for a period in which it was easier to erase the desire for a people's emancipation. This futile hope

---

40　Camus, *Le Premier homme*, 939. My translation and emphasis. Shortly after Camus's death, among the wreckage of the accident, a yellow notebook was found in which he had been jotting down notes and outlines for his novel; this fragment appears in the appendix.

for a return to the past is expressed by a settler portrayed as being reasonable: 'and then we will begin living among men again',[41] a remark that presupposes a highly idealized vision of the colonial past.

Another invocation of a past that is equally mythical, but far more distant: the title itself, which insinuates the idea that no other man was present on this land before him. He is Cormery, he is the European of Algeria, he is *Adam*.[42] This past is like a negating paradise. The central character, Jacques, Camus's alter ego (whom he sometimes calls Albert in his notes), is described as 'born on a land without ancestors and without memory … where old age found none of the consolations of melancholy that it receives in civilized countries'.[43] Let us note immediately that Algeria is not conceived as a 'civilized country'. Yet this is a revealing paradox of a certain privilege, for although formed and educated by the values of what he calls a civilized country, Jacques also perceives himself as part of nature:

He – like a solitary wave, always quivering, destined to be shattered in a single blow and forever – a pure passion for living confronted with a total death; felt today life, youth, human beings slipping away from him, without being able in any way to save them, abandoned solely to the blind hope that the obscure force which for so many years had lifted him above the days, nourished him without measure, equal to the harshest of circumstances, would also provide him – with the same tireless generosity with which it had given him his reasons for living – with reasons to grow old and to die without revolt.[44]

41　Ibid., 852.

42　Camus considered replacing the given name 'Jacques' with 'Adam': 'in fact I would have preferred to give him [Cormery] another name, Adam'. See Albert Camus, *Œuvres complètes*, vol. IV, 'Notice', n. 3, interview with *Il gazzettino*, 9 July 1959, 1522.

43　Ibid., 914–15.

44　Ibid.

This 'obscure force' is a regression towards an infantile temporality that turns Jacques into a wave (a 'blade'): this fusion with nature, which had allowed the colonial realities to be obscured, is disturbed by the forces of history. The principal drama of the man who unconsciously fashioned himself as the first man of Algeria lies in this new impossibility of disregarding the Other.

This dream of a return to the colonial past is shattered; the fantasy of the pieds-noirs as indigenous to Algeria, maintained by Camus ('The French of Algeria are also, in the strong sense of the term, indigenous'[45]), is dismantled by the Algerian people themselves. Camus's personal disarray and incomprehension are commensurate with the imminence of the French defeat on the ground.

One understands, then, that the anonymous Algerian shot by Meursault (for having violated the privileged space of his communion with the sea and the sun) met his death also because he embodied the inevitability of History – independence! – whose beginnings in 1954 form the backdrop to *The First Man*; the text reveals itself as the heartfelt cry of a writer who, compelled by events, ultimately lays bare to the world the extent of his attachment to his identity as a settler.

His attachment was such that in May 1958, four years after the outbreak of the Algerian War of Independence, he wrote in his *Notebooks*: 'My vocation is to write books and to fight whenever the freedom of those closest to me and of my people is threatened, that is all.'[46] *The First Man* emerges as the synthesis of this double duty: it is, in fact, the novel of a colonial writer.

<hr>

45 Albert Camus, 'Algérie 1958', in *Actuelles, III, Chroniques algériennes, Œuvres complètes*, vol. IV, Paris: Gallimard, 2008, 389.
46 Camus, *Carnets*, in *Œuvres complètes*, vol. IV, 1275.

5

Receptions

The white race no longer has the right to debate the death penalty, since it has trampled and violated every principle that could serve, in this matter, as a point of reference or a standard.

And besides, what would be the point? Even if the death penalty were abolished in law, it would continue to reign in our mores – or rather, through the widespread use of police killing everywhere, which, by comparison, restores to the death penalty a semblance of dignity and honour.

You may strike it from every statute in which it still exists; innocents will nonetheless continue to be legally shot 'for having attempted to flee'.

– François Mauriac[1]

Equivocations on the Guillotine

How many times, under the *Ancien Régime*, was an aristocrat convicted and executed for the murder of a peasant? One might just as well ask how many times – in the entire history of France's occupation of Algeria – a settler was sentenced to have his 'head severed in a public square in the name of the French people'. The historian Alain Ruscio is explicit:

But when was such a sentence not merely carried out, but even contemplated with any degree of plausibility in colonial Algeria?

---

1 François Mauriac, *Le Bloc-Notes 1952–1962*, Paris: Robert Laffont, 2020, 423. My translation.

The answer is: *never*. During more than a century of presence, cases of unpunished murders of natives were numerous. Not a single capital sentence was applied to a European for this type of crime. By contrast, Muslims guillotined numbered in the hundreds.[2]

The entire narrative structure of the second part of *The Stranger*, therefore, rests on a mystification. Camus was in a better position than anyone to know this: as a court reporter for *Alger républicain*, a careful observer of many trials, a regular attendee at the criminal court, he could not have been unaware of the implausible nature of *The Stranger*'s judicial scenario. Why, then, this obsession with the death penalty, a recurring theme throughout almost all of his work?

Mauriac's answer, for his part, is unequivocal: 'Discussing the death penalty, I fear, spares beautiful souls from confronting more pressing problems.'[3]

Indeed, Camus – reluctant to speak of systems or ideology – preferred moralism, 'noble phrases', and 'elevated sentiments'.[4] Depending on the period and the stakes involved, he was sometimes for, somsetimes against (though always with qualifications) the death penalty. Contrary to what contemporary reception – which casts him as an almost prophetic abolitionist – might suggest, his commitments on this issue were intermittent and contradictory.

---

2   A comprehensive survey finds that between 1843 – the date of the first use of the guillotine in Algeria – and the eve of the Algerian War, there were 361 capital executions of Muslims, an average of three per year. Over the same period, twenty-one Europeans were executed, all for crimes committed against other Europeans (see guillotine.voila. net). Alain Ruscio, 'Albert Camus and Algeria: Passions, engagements, hésitations, renoncements', *Nejma*, January 2018, p. 10. My translation.

3   Mauriac, *Le Bloc-Notes 1952–1962*, 424.

4   Simone de Beauvoir, *La Force des choses*, in *Mémoires*, vol. I, Paris: Gallimard, 2018, 992.

In Favour of Purges

At first, Camus supported the death penalty in an article entitled 'Tout ne s'arrange pas' (All is not well), published in *Les Lettres françaises*, the clandestine journal of the CNE. He explains that Pierre Pucheu, a member of the Vichy government, was executed because he had 'lacked imagination'. For Camus, Pucheu failed to grasp that this government was 'not like the others'; nonetheless, he still deserved the death penalty:

> We now know that, in the world we inhabit, one thing is equivalent to death, and that is a lack of imagination. No one has the right to lack it any longer … It must be known throughout France (and in every ministry) that the age of abstraction is over. Everything now has meaning, and that meaning can be deadly. That is the truth one can draw from the execution of Pierre Pucheu … But it is in the full light of imagination that we learn at the same time – and through a paradox that is only apparent – to accept without revolt that a man can be erased from the earth. For what is at work here is not the judgement of a class or an ideology, not a verdict pronounced in the name of an abstraction. It is the general cry, the call, a language full of flesh and real images, the demand of all of us who have been defendants for four years, suddenly strong enough to judge our judges ourselves, and to do so without hatred, *but without mercy*.[5]

Rare enough to merit mention, Camus's convoluted article was followed by an editorial clarification insisting on the deliberate nature of Pucheu's actions. It seems clear that Camus's contortions – if not his indulgence – regarding Pucheu's supposed motivations caused discomfort:

---

5 Albert Camus, 'Tout ne s'arrange pas', *Les Lettres françaises*, no. 16 (May 1944): 1. My translation and emphasis.

In response to the article 'Nothing Gets Sorted Out', which may be read elsewhere, several of our friends, while agreeing with the author's general thesis, nevertheless wish to state that this so convenient lack of imagination he refers to seems to them always – and particularly in the case of Pierre Pucheu – to have been deliberate. It is deliberately that a criminal like Pucheu, driven above all by the desire to satisfy his hatreds, has no conscience.[6]

Immediately after this brief reprimand, from May 1944 to January 1945, Camus would no longer write for *Les Lettres françaises*, and his support for capital punishment became more emphatic. In an article dated 4 May 1944, attributed to him and bearing the striking title 'For Three Hours They Shot Frenchmen', the editorialist – seeking to convince *Combat*'s readers of the necessity of the death penalty for collaborators – writes:

This is the image that must be kept before our eyes so that nothing is forgotten, the image that must be shown to all French people who still stand aside. For among these eighty-six innocents, many believed that since they had done nothing against the German force, nothing would be done to them. But France is indivisible; there is only one anger, only one martyrdom … For the question is not whether these crimes will be forgiven, but whether they will be paid for. And if we were tempted to doubt it, the image of this village soaked in blood and now populated only by widows and orphans would suffice to assure us that the crime will be paid for, since this now depends on all French people, and since, *in the face of this new massacre, we discover in ourselves the solidarity of martyrdom and the forces of vengeance.*[7]

---

6   Ibid.

7   Albert Camus, 'Pendant trois heures ils ont fusillé des français', *Combat*, n. 57 (May 1944). My translation and emphasis.

His vehemence and enthusiasm shock Mauriac, an authentic intellectual resister, who openly criticized him in an editorial in *Le Figaro*. Camus replied forcefully, giving rise to a public controversy that would last several months. Let us remove any ambiguity: *Combat*'s editorialist was in favour of the death penalty; *Le Figaro*'s was against it.

Throughout the final six months of 1944, Camus conducted a veritable campaign of editorials (in *Combat*) in support of capital punishment. In light of his later mythologization as a herald of abolition, his words now strike a discordant note: on 18 October 1944, 'the issue is not to purge extensively, but to purge properly';[8] on the 21st, 'when we are tempted to prefer to the dark labours of justice the generous sacrifices of war, we will need the memory of the dead';[9] on the 25th, 'We desire … the immediate repression of the most obvious crimes, and then, since nothing can be done without mediocrity, the reasoned forgetting of the errors that so many French people nevertheless committed.' On 2 November, he exhorted his readers: 'Demand the most pitiless and resolute justice.'[10]

Given Camus's later position, it is important to note that the driving force of his reasoning – which unfolded relentlessly in the public arena over several months – was fuelled by anger, by a spirit of reprisal, and by vengeance.

Against Purges

At first, Camus remained faithful to his earlier positions. When Simone de Beauvoir explained her refusal to intervene on Robert Brasillach's behalf, she cited, among other things, Camus's similar stance:

---

8   *Combat*, 18 October 1944, 76–8.
9   *Combat*, 21 October 1944, 82–3.
10   Camus, 'Pendant trois heures ils ont fusillés des français', 5–6.

If I had lifted a finger in favour of Brasillach, I would have deserved to be spat at in the face. I did not hesitate for a moment; the question did not even arise. Camus had the same reaction: 'We have nothing to do with people like that,' he told me. 'The judges will decide; it's none of our business.'[11]

Shortly after the trial, under the auspices of, among others, Thierry Maulnier,[12] a prestigious committee was formed to request clemency for the poet and virulent collaborator from de Gaulle. It included Anouilh, Aymé, Claudel, Cocteau, Colette, Paulhan, Valéry – and Mauriac. Camus then reversed his position on the death penalty: he joined the committee and signed the petition. (He would later also intervene on behalf of Lucien Rebatet, another notorious collaborator and the author of *Mémoires d'un fasciste*.[13])

Was Camus an Abolitionist?

The contemporary reception of Camus, made up of constant praise and celebration, leaves little room for addressing the ambiguities of his positions on capital punishment. The reference work, with its strikingly reductive title – *Camus against*

---

11   Simone de Beauvoir, *Mémoires*, vol. I, Paris: Gallimard, 2018, 822. My translation.

12   Thierry Maulnier, in *L'Action française* of 2 February 1943, wrote a long, laudatory review of *L'Étranger* and *Le Mythe de Sisyphe*: 'We are in the presence of one of the most significant literary debuts of recent years.' Mauriac would later remind *Figaro* readers of Thierry Maulnier's antisemitism and affiliation with *L'Action française*. Maulnier became a major figure in French literary criticism after the war and publicly supported the execution of French Communist and pro-Algerian independence activist Fernand Iveton. In Jean-Luc Einaudi, *Pour l'exemple: l'affaire Ferand Iveton*, Paris: l'Harmattan, 1986, 200.

13   Rebatet was sentenced to death in 1946 but pardoned the following year.

the Death Penalty[14] – is entirely devoted to his glorification. Its preface was written by Robert Badinter, who, as minister of justice in 1981, introduced the bill abolishing the death penalty in France. What does he say about Camus? First, that Camus was always opposed to capital punishment: 'That the refusal of the death penalty was, throughout his life, a founding principle for Camus is what Ève Morisi's book brings to light.' This claim runs through the entire preface, up to its highly lyrical conclusion: 'Thus, until the brutal and premature end of his earthly existence, Albert Camus never ceased to combat the death penalty.' One also finds an equally laudatory but imprecise comparison: 'Like Victor Hugo, this struggle is a golden thread running through the fabric of his life.'[15]

In this preface – perhaps even more troubling than the omission of Camus's public positions during the year 1944 – we are told that Camus systematically responded favourably to requests from Gisèle Halimi and others seeking support for petitions for clemency for FLN militants during the War of Independence, through 'letters and approaches addressed to President René Coty or to the President of the Council, Guy Mollet'.[16] Yet, in certain cases, Camus refused to intervene to prevent the execution of a condemned prisoner. Halimi states this explicitly in her autobiography *Le Lait de l'oranger*:

> Once again, I wanted Camus to intervene with Coty, the Élysée, or some other government official. Mohammed Ben Hamdi had to be granted clemency, and I needed Camus's support. At the same moment, he seemed to be beginning his great silence on Algeria: 'I despise killers of women and children.' That day, he refused me all assistance. Briefly and without ceremony.[17]

---

14 Ève Morisi, *Albert Camus contre la peine de mort*, Paris: Gallimard, 2011.

15 Robert Badinter, 'Preface', in *Albert Camus contre la peine de mort*, i–vi.

16 Badinter, 'Preface', vi.

17 Gisèle Halimi, *Le Lait de l'oranger*, Paris: Gallimard, 1988, 193.

Halimi explains that, after receiving the Nobel Prize, Camus 'no longer intervened at the Élysée on behalf of my Algerian death-row prisoners ... Between us, the matter was settled.'[18]

Camus's opposition to the death penalty was therefore conditional: he refused to intervene on behalf of those he regarded as terrorists. He believed that, for certain individuals, clemency was unwarranted and that the death penalty was justified in some cases. Far from being an abolitionist, Camus appoints himself judge before agreeing – if at all – to support a request for clemency.

Reversals on the Death Penalty

Yet in *Reflections on the Guillotine* (1957),[19] Camus presents himself as an abolitionist, declaring himself opposed to the death penalty in general and to the guillotine in particular. He assigns himself a task: to refute the arguments in favour of capital punishment. Is the guillotine a swift, even humane, means of execution? Camus cites medical reports, the recollections of executioners, and the testimony of a prison chaplain to describe in precise detail the effects of an execution. According to the conclusions of a paper presented to the Academy of Medicine, the decapitated do not die immediately. According to the chaplain at La Santé Prison, whom Camus quotes at length, a decapitated prisoner 'answered when his name was called'.[20] After a long, highly detailed account of the horrors of the guillotine, Camus sets out to refute the idea that the death penalty has a deterrent effect: 'All statistics without exception ... show that there is no link between the abolition of the death penalty and criminality.'[21] If it is not a deterrent, what purpose does capital

---

18 Ibid., 202.

19 Albert Camus, *Réflexions sur la guillotine*, in *Œuvres complètes*, vol. IV, 125–67. My translations.

20 Ibid., 134.

21 Ibid., 139.

punishment serve? Camus answers in a declamatory tone: 'Let us call it by its name, which, for lack of any other nobility, at least give it that of truth, so let us recognize it for what it fundamentally is: an act of vengeance.'[22] It should be noted that, in his *Reflections*, Camus says nothing about his own calls for vengeance in *Combat*, which were intended to sustain the spirit of revenge against high-level collaborators among his readers. He does cite the Brasillach case, but without detailing his own changing positions, leaving the misleading impression of a man who opposed the death penalty during the purge.

Camus continues his indictment: one of the principal causes of murders, he argues, is alcohol abuse. Citing statistics, he points the finger at the shareholders of an 'aperitif company' and at the deputies who passed laws in their favour: 'They have certainly killed more children than they think.' Camus's proposed solution: 'to begin with, it seems to me indispensable and urgent to take them [the deputies and shareholders], under military escort, to the next execution of a child killer'.[23]

At the end of his *Reflections*, Camus suggests a compromise. What he ultimately detests most is the method rather than the execution itself; he would like 'science' to be able 'at least to serve to kill decently'. He therefore proposes an 'anaesthetic' to restore a measure of 'decency' in place of a 'sordid and obscene exhibition'. This 'anaesthetic' would be made available to the condemned 'for at least a day, so that he might use it freely'.[24] Buried in these somewhat hazy societal considerations, almost in passing, one can nonetheless find – if one looks carefully – a link to a far more concrete current event: 'the Fernand Iveton affair', even though Camus does not mention his name.

Camus's *Reflections* were written in the midst of the War of Independence, during the Battle of Algiers. The context was that of terrorist attacks in Algeria launched by a pro–French

---

22   Ibid., 143.
23   Ibid., 150.
24   Ibid., 167.

Algeria anti-independence commando who managed to enter the Casbah, exclusively populated with Algerians and then under siege. No doubt with the complicity of the French army, the commando committed the infamous massacre on Rue de Thèbes on 10 August 1956, which left more than eighty dead among the civilian population, and dozens wounded.

Five months after the Rue de Thèbes bombing, Fernand Iveton, a French Algerian and Communist militant, planted a bomb in his factory. He did not want to cause any casualties; this is an established fact, as Sartre would later write in *Les Temps modernes*:

> In November 1956, Fernand Iveton ... planted a bomb on the premises of the Hamma power station. An attempt at sabotage that cannot, under any circumstances, be equated to an act of terrorism: expert examination established that it was a timed device, meticulously set so that the explosion could not occur before the staff had left. None of this mattered: Iveton was arrested, sentenced to death, denied clemency, and executed. Not the slightest hesitation: this man declared and proved that he wanted no one's death, but we wanted his, and we obtained it without weakness.[25]

Between his arrest (14 November 1956) and his execution (7 February 1957), few people spoke out in an attempt to save him.

According to the historian Alain Ruscio, the writer Emmanuel Roblès, a close friend of Camus, sought his help: 'contacted by Roblès to intervene on behalf of the condemned man, [Camus] refused'.[26] Given his prestige and his status as a French Algerian, Camus's intervention would undoubtedly have been

---

25 Jean-Paul Sartre, 'Nous sommes tous des assassins', *Les Temps modernes*, March 1958. Cited in *Situations V*, Paris: Gallimard, 1964, 68. My translation.

26 Alain Ruscio, *Les Communistes et l'Algérie*, Paris: La Découverte, 2019, 34.

decisive (moreover, he maintained cordial relations with the minister of justice at the time, François Mitterrand).[27] Camus's failure to intervene on Iveton's behalf can also be read between the lines of the book by Stora and Malye on Mitterrand during the War of Independence: in the section dealing with Iveton, one of the authors notes that, as a guest of Camus's daughter in his former residence in Lourmarin, he was able, 'standing at the lectern of the Nobel Prize winner in literature, to leaf through the letters he had sent pleading for clemency for certain prisoners sentenced to death'.[28] There is no mention of Fernand Iveton.

In his notebooks, Emmanuel Roblès recounts a meeting with Camus shortly after Iveton's execution:

> Lunch with Camus at Lipp. At the end: 'the Iveton tragedy', he told me, 'perhaps soon yours'. He meant to say that some French Algerians were giving in to the desire to prove to Algerians that they were separating themselves from their compatriots, the colonialist French, the 'Ultras' as we called them. To prove that we were not on the side of the oppressors, that we would deserve, once freedom was won, to live with the formerly oppressed in a brotherhood never severed. But according to Camus, Iveton's bomb featured among such 'proofs'.[29]

No sympathy on Camus's part towards Iveton can be detected.

Curiously, in the absence of any documentation establishing a gesture by Camus in Iveton's favour (a letter, a signature), and

---

27 Camus inscribed a dedication of his play *Les Justes* to François Mitterrand with the following wording: 'To the Minister of the Interior, in remembrance of a just cause, and with the deferential homage of Albert Camus'. Mitterrand was minister of the interior from June 1954 to February 1955, and minister of justice starting on 1 February 1957; Iveton was executed on 11 February of that same year.

28 François Malye and Benjamin Stora, *François Mitterrand et la guerre d'Algérie*, Paris: Calmann-Lévy, 2010, 202.

29 Catherine Brun and Olivier Penot-Lacassagne, *Engagements et Déchirements les intellectuels et la guerre d'Algérie*, Paris: Gallimard, 2012, 103. My translation.

in the absence of any testimony, contemporary criticism none-theless assumes that such a gesture took place. In the *Œuvres complètes*, a note informs us that 'it seems that he intervened', only to qualify this immediately: 'in any case, he remained haunted by Yveton [sic]'. Even in the novel that rehabilitates Iveton, *Tomorrow They Won't Dare to Murder Us*, André Abbou[30] – cited by the author – provides no concrete evidence, but imagines, on the penultimate page, that Camus 'may have intervened in an attempt to save him'.[31]

Today, it is rare to see a frank and lucid assessment of Camus's ambiguities on the death penalty; this was not always the case. In July 1957, when Camus's book was published, Mauriac experienced a distinct unease. For the author of *Thérèse Desqueyroux*, to hold forth on capital punishment in the midst of the Algerian War – at a time when torture was being systematically practised by French forces – was Camus's way of sidestepping the issue. In the columns of *L'Express*, Mauriac told him directly:

> The death penalty: abolishing it should be the crowning achieve-ment of legislation that no military or civilian police force would have the power to violate. We know what the situation is to-day … Abolish the death penalty while restoring torture? *Let's have a little logic, Camus!*[32]

He would say it again in 1958:

---

30 André Abbou, who – as we have seen – considers the designation 'Arabs' in Camus's work to be a mark of respect.

31 Cited in Joseph Andras, *De nos frères blessés*, Arles: Actes Sud, 2016, 139. My emphasis. In the English translation, *Tomorrow They Won't Dare to Murder US*, London and New York: Verso, 2021, 136, Abbou's conditional statement is no longer quoted but introduced as a claim.

32 Mauriac, *Le Bloc-Notes 1952–1962*, 424–5. My translations and emphasis.

One must be either thoroughly hypocritical or completely blind to believe that it is the death penalty that we are being enjoined to explain ourselves about … to abolish the death penalty … is an honour we must earn … by troubling ourselves with what has become of the several thousand people who have disappeared into that darkness in which we search for Maurice Audin.[33]

The major cause célèbre of the period 1954–62 was opposition to the systematic use of torture against pro-independence militants by the French state through its army.[34] This was a practice that Camus did not address and that he refused to condemn publicly. The torturers, for their part, had nothing to fear from the justice system, since they fell under the authority of military tribunals and were protected by the French executive branch. Torture was denounced from the very beginning of the War of Independence in 1954, but the publication of Henri Alleg's testimonial book in February 1958, *The Question*,[35] written from military prison, was electrifying.[36] *L'Express*, which published Sartre's article celebrating the book ('A Victory'[37]) on 6 March 1958, was immediately seized. All press outlets that reported on it were likewise censored. The book was banned on 27 March.

---

33   Ibid., 524. Maurice Audin (1932–57), a young pied-noir, professor of mathematics at the University of Algiers, anti-colonialist activist, and member of the Algerian Communist Party (PCA), was suspected of supporting the FLN; arrested on 11 June 1957, he was tortured and killed during his interrogation by French paratroopers on the orders of General Aussaresses. See 'Les aveux posthumes du général Aussaresses: "On a tué Audin"', francetvinfo.fr, 9 January 2014.

34   As for the use of torture, 'it was tolerated, if not recommended', explains General Paul Aussaresses – cf. *Services spéciaux: Algérie, 1955–57*, Paris: Perrin, 2001, 89.

35   Henri Alleg, *La Question* (originally published in 1958), Paris: Éditions de Minuit, 2008.

36   As early as January of 1955, Claude Bourdet (*France-Observateur*) and François Mauriac (*L'Express*) denounced the use of torture in Algeria.

37   Sartre, *Situations V*, 88.

In April, Jérôme Lindon, head of Éditions de Minuit, which had published the book, approached Sartre, Malraux, and three Nobel Prize–winning writers – Camus, Roger Martin du Gard, and Mauriac – to ask them to sign an 'Address to the President of the Republic'[38] condemning torture and censorship. Why ask for a signature from Malraux, who by now was close to the Gaullists, and, to a lesser extent, from Martin du Gard, who was highly reluctant to engage in public interventions? One initial answer might be that opposition to torture constituted a second political fault line. Indeed, some figures whose positions on Algerian independence were equivocal nevertheless clearly condemned torture – notably Malraux, but also the Christian existentialist Gabriel Marcel, as well as the publisher Roland Laudenbach of Éditions de la Table Ronde, despite his pronounced right-wing leanings.

It should be noted that this solemn appeal was a 'protest' against censorship and against 'all seizures and infringements on freedom of expression', and also a public petition (to be signed and returned to the Ligue des droits de l'Homme) demanding from the government an 'unequivocal condemnation of the use of torture'.[39] There was nothing radical about it: merely a minimal commitment against torture and censorship in what was then called the new Dreyfus Affair.

Mauriac and Sartre accepted immediately. Martin du Gard and Malraux hesitated for a time. In the end, all agreed to sign – except Camus, who attempted to explain his refusal in a carefully worded letter to Jérôme Lindon:

> More than a year ago, after recognizing what separated me definitively from both the Left and the Right on the Algerian question, I decided no longer to associate myself with any public campaign on this subject ... Even when the objective

---

38 'Protestation contre la saisie de *La Question* d'Henri Alleg', *L'Express*, 17 April 1958: 2.
39 Ibid.

is valid – and it is here – I therefore decided to act only on a personal basis.[40]

Halimi, who stood on the front lines of the legal struggle against the death penalty and torture, would speak of Camus's tightrope-walking qualities: for her, he had become a 'moral acrobat'.[41]

Camus and Women: All Except My Mother

The French novelist and philosopher Albert Camus was a ter-rifically good-looking guy whom women fell for helplessly – the Don Draper of existentialism.

– Adam Gopnik[42]

The current enthusiasm for Camus as a great humanist con-science is not confined to his texts on the guillotine – far from it. With regard to his relationship to women, as well, the con-trast between Camus's writings and their reception in France is striking.

Shortly before her death, Maria Casarès – the great actress of French cinema and theatre – sold the letters Camus had sent her over nearly fifteen years to Camus's daughter. The latter now possesses a complete, two-way correspondence – a 'rarity'.

Published in October 2017, this correspondence immedi-ately sparked intense excitement in the mainstream press. The letters were described as 'sublime',[43] as 'lessons in writing';[44]

---

40   Alexis Berchadsky, *'La Question' d'Henri Alleg: Un livre-événement dans la France en guerre d'Algérie (juin 1957–juin 1958)*, Paris: Larousse, 1994, 128–9. My translation.

41   Halimi, *Le Lait de l'oranger*, 204. My translation.

42   Adam Gopnik, 'Facing History', *The New Yorker*, 9 April 2012.

43   Jean-Paul Enthoven, *Le Point,* 23 November 2017.

44   Maurice Szafran, 'D'amour et de lettres: 15 ans d'échanges admirables entre Casarès et Camus', *Challenges*, 19 November 2017.

they were said to be 'swollen with a radiant love',[45] to constitute 'a bracing surprise',[46] to be 'rich and intense' (*Le Matin*).
They were said to tell a story 'now destined to enter legend'
(*Challenges*); for others, the correspondence was simply 'phe-
nomenal' (*Le Temps*). Moreover, in the introduction to the
hefty volume – more than 800 letters, over a thousand pages –
we are informed that, thanks to these letters, 'the earth is vaster,
space more luminous, the air lighter'.[47]

We also learn that it supposedly shattered records for the
genre, and that Isabelle Adjani and Lambert Wilson are set to
read some of these famous letters at literary evenings – we are
warned in advance: 'it will be a riot to get in'.[48] Other actors
will likewise give public readings of this kind.[49]

Yet when set against this disproportionate fervour, the actual
reading of the correspondence is surprising. In virtually every
letter, Camus complains, most often about his own fate – to
the point that Casarès comes to write: 'one thing troubles me
… your bouts of discouragement whenever work does not go
exactly the way you want it to'.[50] He also complains about
Casarès's letters, finding them 'not long enough, not warm
enough'.[51] Married to Francine, Camus does not want Casarès
to forget him, and believes the best way to ensure this is for her
to remain alone. For example, in the summer of 1949, when

---

45   Frédérique Roussel, 'Le don de l'amour: correspondance de
Casarès et Camus', *Libération*, 4–5 November 2017.

46   Estelle Lenartowicz, 'Albert Camus et Maria Casarès: l'amour
jusqu'au bout', *L'Express*, 22 November 2017.

47   Albert Camus and Maria Casarès, 'Avant-propos by Catherine
Camus', in *Correspondance (1944–1959)*, Paris: Gallimard, 2021, 10.

48   *Le Point*, 13 July 2018.

49   The idea was also taken up for Camus's *Notebooks* – his
private journals – which an actor read aloud. The correspondence
inspired a new biography of Casarès.

50   Albert Camus's Letter to M. Casarès, *Correspondance*, Letter
158, 332. My translations.

51   Casarès, *Correspondance*, Letter 327, 663.

he was in Brazil and she was in France, Camus bombarded Casarès in nearly every letter with his 'worries', imploring her to reassure him and asking for letters with ever greater frequency. On 17 July, he also spelled out the course of action she should follow should she accept an invitation to the *Festival du film maudit* in Biarritz, which Jean Cocteau, Raymond Queneau, and Robert Bresson would attend:

> I have no opinion about Biarritz ... Personally, when I am far from you, I have only one desire as far as you are concerned: to know you are locked in your room, double bolted, until my arrival ... Only he who has dreamed of perpetual imprisonment for the woman he cherishes has truly loved.[52]

If, by chance, Casarès mentions in a letter a man who worries Camus, he hastens to warn her:

> From your letter received at noon, I retained only one thing – that lunch [with Jean Servais] – and I spent a very hard day and a difficult night ... You must know that I would stop at nothing to destroy anything in you that is not – or has not been – mine, just as I would be capable of the worst things in order to keep you.[53]

Camus also demands detailed accounts of Casarès's activities (as a result, for a time, she kept a sort of diary for him), and he sometimes takes offence when she goes out in the evening: 'What is the point of going to bed so late, especially in Switzerland, and without me?'[54]

Sexual jealousy did not begin with his relationship with Casarès (which started on 6 June 1944). It is, in fact, a central theme in Camus's work. In his first novel, *A Happy Death*, long unpublished and released only posthumously in 1970, an entire chapter is devoted to it. Patrice Mersault goes to the cinema

---

52   Casarès, *Correspondance*, Letter 71, 146.
53   Casarès, *Correspondance*, Letter 338, 681.
54   Casarès, *Correspondance*, Letter 623, 1122.

with Marthe and catches sight of one of her former lovers, a presence to which he reacts in a striking manner:

> Mersault felt everything collapse within him, and behind his closed eyes, as the bell in the cinema announced the resumption of the show, tears of rage swelled. He forgot Marthe, who had been merely the pretext for his joy and was now the living embodiment of his anger.[55]

This conception of women – whose independent existence irritates Camus to the highest degree – reappears twenty years later in his notes for his final novel, *The First Man*, where he explains that he does not want the women he desires to have a past: 'Loves: he would have wanted them all to be virgins of past and of men.'[56] As for the others, those he does not desire, they bore him. This viewpoint haunts his writing. In his *Notebooks* in 1942, he asserts that 'a woman, outside of love, is boring. She does not know. One must live with one and keep silent. Or sleep with all of them and act. What matters most lies elsewhere.'[57] This other Camusian axiom resurfaces in his fiction, for example in *The Fall*, where Clamence expresses

---

55 Albert Camus, *La mort heureuse*, in *Cahiers Albert Camus*, vol. I, Paris: Gallimard, 1971, 53–4. My translations.

56 Albert Camus, *Le Premier homme*, in *Œuvres complètes*, vol. IV, 315. This refusal of women's autonomy, this desire to erase their past – indeed, their very existence prior to their conquest – that is, before he 'possesses' them, to use Camus's own terminology – closely parallels a certain colonial logic in relation to Algeria: a tendency found in Camus, of course, and extending all the way to Macron, which culminates in denying the very existence of Algeria prior to the French invasion. Camus himself draws this parallel between his relationship to women and to Algeria in his *Notebooks* in January 1943, when he compared his (ambiguous) relationship to the metropole with that to French Algeria: 'As for Algeria, by contrast, it is unbridled passion and a surrender to the sensuous pleasure of love. Question: can a country be loved as one loves a woman?' Albert Camus, *Œuvres complètes*, vol. II, Paris: Gallimard, 2006, 980. My translation.

57 In Camus, *Œuvres complètes*, vol. II, 970. My translation.

Camus's own thinking: 'Outside of desire, women bored me beyond all expectation, and, visibly, I bored them as well.'[58]

In the most disturbing passage of *The Fall* – a narrative whose words are often said to resemble a confession by Camus himself – Clamence boasts of his revenge against a woman who had dared to criticize his sexual performance. He recounts his encounter with this anonymous woman who had 'attracted [him] by her passive and avid manner':

> It was mediocre, as was to be expected … I thought she had noticed nothing, and it never even occurred to me that she might have an opinion … Yet a few weeks later I learned that she had confided my inadequacies to a third party … Some time afterward I saw this woman again; I did what was necessary to seduce her and truly take her back … From that moment on, without clearly intending it, I began in fact to humiliate her in every possible way. I abandoned her and took her back; I forced her to give herself at times and in places wholly unsuited to it; I treated her so brutally, in every respect, that I ended up becoming attached to her, as I imagine a jailer becomes attached to his prisoner. And this went on until the day when, in the violent disorder of a painful and constrained pleasure, she paid loud homage to that which enslaved her. That day, I began to distance myself from her. Since then, I have forgotten her.[59]

A curious echo of this particular conception of sexual relations can be found in Camus's reaction to the publication of *The Second Sex*, as Simone de Beauvoir recounts in *The Force of Things*:

> Camus accused me, in a few morose sentences, of having ridiculed the French male. A Mediterranean man, cultivating a Spanish pride, he conceded to women only equality in

---

58   Camus, *La chute*, in *Œuvres* complètes, vol. III, 743. My translation.

59   Ibid., 725–6.

difference, and obviously, as George Orwell would have put it, he was the more equal of the two. He had once cheerfully admitted to us that he found it hard to bear the idea of being assessed, judged by a woman: she was the object; he the consciousness and the gaze; he laughed about it – but it was true that he did not accept reciprocity. He concluded with a sudden warmth: 'There was an argument you should have put forward: man himself suffers from not finding in woman a true companion; he longs for equality.' He too preferred a cry from the heart to reason – and, to cap it all, uttered in the name of men. Most of them took what I had reported about female frigidity as a personal insult; they liked to imagine that they dispensed pleasure at will; to doubt it was to castrate them.[60]

For Camus, women exist to be observed, admired, loved (by him alone); outside of this, they serve no purpose – unlike men. A passage from *A Happy Death* illustrates this conception, which recurs throughout his work: 'But what of it? A man's beauty embodies inner and practical truths. His face reveals what he is capable of doing. And what does that amount to compared with the magnificent uselessness of a woman's face?'[61]

One may describe his relationship to women as adversarial. In his *Notebooks*, a watchword appears: 'To renounce the servitude of female attraction.'[62] Very early on, Camus theorized his misogyny as a form of liberation, for example in *The Myth of Sisyphus*. Camus's theory of the absurd man's relations with women corresponds in no way to the image one forms of the author when reading his contemporaneous critics (very much including those who wrote about his correspondence with Casarès). *The Myth of Sisyphus* is also a catalogue of examples of absurd lives. For once the absurd has been explained, one

<hr>

60   Simone de Beauvoir, *La Force des choses*, 1132.
61   Camus, *La mort heureuse*, 52.
62   Camus, *Carnets 1935–48*, in *Œuvres complètes*, vol. II, 922.

must show how to live an absurd life; that is, a life lived in full awareness of the absurdity of existence. Don Juan is an absurd man for Camus, one of his great models. For the absurd man is an individualist. He is free from the common laws that apply to ordinary mortals. He operates within a logic of living *more* rather than living *better*. What defines the absurd man is a determination to privilege an ethics of 'quantity' over 'quality', especially where women are concerned. No great love then: 'Not to believe in the deeper meaning of things is the mark of the absurd man.' One must move quickly; there is no time to lose: 'For the man who seeks the quantity of joys, efficiency alone counts.' Presenting himself as an expert in conquest, Camus explains his 'sacrifices' and the fact that his life tends towards a 'fierce denouement of an existence devoted to joys without tomorrows'.[63]

Far from that lyrical conclusion, in the week following his accidental death, the three loves of his life at that moment in time – Maria Casarès, Catherine Sellers, and Mette Ivers – received letters from their lover announcing his return to Paris. The grandiose eloquence of his early declarations gives way to the melodrama of a bourgeois marriage. Yet this correspondence, which reveals a morbid jealousy and a pathological desire for control, has, as we have seen, enjoyed a rapturous reception. This can be explained in part by the fact that Camus represents a financial windfall for his publishers and rights holders:

Nine million copies of *The Stranger* (translated into seventy languages) and 4.7 million copies of *The Plague* have to date been sold in France, which makes Camus, with more than twenty million ... in the Folio [paperback] series, the number one bestselling author in the collection.[64]

63 *Le Mythe de Sisyphe*, in *Œuvres complètes*, vol. I, 266–9.
64 Marianne Payot, 'L'écrivain: La corne d'abondance de Gallimard', *L'Express*, 24 December 2019.

During his lifetime, Camus was by no means naïve about the motives of his publisher, for whom he worked and whom, in his correspondence with Casarès, he referred to as the 'Gallimard conglomerate'.[65] It is therefore by reading his own words – his works and, here, his letters – that one discovers the multiple facets of the man, which contradict the mythic image that has been constructed of the handsome novelist: upright, solitary, committed to solidarity, tormented yet just.

Contrary to these public portraits, his correspondence reveals a man utterly crushed by the controversy surrounding *The Rebel* and by the break with Sartre – a falling out that amounted to a true public humiliation from which he recovered only with difficulty. One grasps the extent of its impact in this letter to Casarès in which he explains that he had resumed work on *The Fall*:

> In any case, my confidence returned. To tell the whole truth, for all these months I had carried such constant anxiety about my capacity for work that this first success, after so many months, was enough for me, once I had written the final word, to burst into tears like an infant.[66]

This discouragement is that of a writer of modest origins who, here, does not brandish them to claim an authority denied to others, but experiences them instead as a lack of confidence – that confidence so often the preserve of the bourgeois classes. In this moment of great vulnerability, it is therefore his class identity that resurfaces.

In another of these moments of epistolary candour, Camus evokes his mother and the inauthentic image he presented of his relationship with her: 'Even my mother, whom I claim to place above everything else. I must admit that I have nothing to say to her.'[67]

---

65 Camus-Casarès, *Correspondance*, Letter 623, 1121.
66 Casarès, *Correspondance*, Letter 668, 1173.
67 Casarès, *Correspondance*, Letter 501, 955.

On reading this celebrated correspondence, if there is any surprise, it is not 'invigorating' but demystifying: one discovers there an ambiguous man, who combined a certain opportunism with many insecurities and a deep-seated sexism.

Yet, in France, Camus is presented as a model, an example to be followed. Beyond staged readings of certain letters to Casarès and selected excerpts from his *Notebooks*, there is also a documentary with an eloquent title – *Living with Camus* – which shows how citizens of the world live and survive thanks to Camus. From vertigo to existential anxiety, via heartbreak, reading Camus is said to be a miracle cure; he is cast as a saviour.

He is also a victim. The common thread running through Camus's popularity among our elites is anti-communism: the notion that Camus is said to have been right, against everyone, about the Soviet Union,[68] and that he was persecuted as a result, has for the moment culminated in a book suggesting that he was assassinated by the KGB, which allegedly sabotaged Michel Gallimard's car. Another work of imagination is the book written by Nicolas Sarkozy's speechwriter, Henri Guaino: *Camus at the Panthéon: An Imagined Speech*. These are only a few examples among many others: television dramas in his honour, films, an opera, and graphic novels. These tributes to Camus amount to attempts – more or less lucrative – to appropriate his legacy.

Daoud Whitewashes Camus

Of all Camus's exegetes, interpreters, and observers, the one who most closely resembles him is undoubtedly Kamel Daoud. His novel *The Meursault Investigation* had the impact of a

---

68 Interventions, notably for Hungary, which François Mauriac described as 'crocodile tears', because it was so obvious that Camus's humanist solicitude applied with far less intensity to the victims of French colonialism. François Mauriac, *Le Bloc-Notes 1952–1962*, Paris: Robert Laffont, 2020, 545.

thunderclap when it appeared in France. Written in the style of *The Fall*, it takes up the narrative thread of *The Stranger*, but from an Algerian point of view: the narrator, Haroun, is the younger brother of the Algerian, hitherto unnamed, killed by Meursault. As in *The Fall*, the narrator addresses a silent interlocutor (we later learn that he is French and an academic). As in *The Fall*, the setting is a bar. Haroun evokes his brother Moussa, shot on a beach by Meursault. The narrative injustice appears to be repaired, the record set straight more than half a century later: the victim is – at last – given a name. And it is precisely this colonial anonymity that Haroun criticises:

> I began that accursed book [*The Stranger*] … Everything was there except the essential thing: Moussa's name! Nowhere. I counted and counted again; the word 'Arab' appeared twenty-five times and not a single first name, for any of us. Nothing at all, my friend.[69]

His brother Moussa died 'in insignificance, like a mere extra'.[70] The narrator, Haroun, points out that in the novel there is not a word for him or for their mother: 'There is no trace of our mourning or of what became of us afterwards. Nothing at all, my friend! … There is enough there to allow oneself a bit of anger, don't you think?'[71] These critical passages alternate with others, more ambiguous, which temper the initial questioning:

> Perhaps the right question, after all, is this: what was *your* hero doing on that beach? Not only that day, but for so long a time – indeed, for a century, to be frank. No, believe me, I am not that kind of person. It matters little to me that he is French and I Algerian.[72]

---

69 Kamel Daoud, *Meursault, contre-enquête*, Arles: Actes Sud, 2014, 140. My translations.
70 Ibid., 20.
71 Ibid., 74.
72 Ibid., 73.

Recent history is neutralized: 'The truth is that Independence merely led each side to switch roles.'[73] The conclusion follows: 'Now it is a finished story.'[74]

From this opposition between the desire for recognition and forgiveness granted, an interpretation emerges, as skillful as it is critical, according to which Moussa's murderer would be Camus himself: 'The book was written by the assassin.'[75] Haroun sustains the ambiguity:

> After Independence, the more I read the books of your hero and retraced the rise of his career as a celebrated writer, the more I felt as though I were pressing my face against the window of a banquet hall to which neither my mother nor I had been invited. Everything happened without us, *even after the death of the murderer.*[76]

The writer as assassin. To make the connection between the murderous novelist and Meursault absolutely clear, Haroun asks his silent interlocutor whether, like Meursault/Camus, 'Moussa had a revolver, *a philosophy, tuberculosis, ideas, or a mother and a justice?*'[77] But the narrator does not stop there! He accuses Camus of attempting genocide when speaking of Oran, the city in which *The Plague* is set: '*It was here, incidentally, that your hero failed when he tried to move from murder to genocide.*'[78]

In the original edition of *The Meursault Investigation*, published in Algiers in 2013, Daoud explicitly draws a link between the fetishized author of a certain left and colonial violence. But neither the metropolitan nor the Anglophone readers will be

---

73 Ibid., 20–1.

74 Ibid., 21.

75 Ibid., 134.

76 Kamel Daoud, *Meursault, contre-enquête*, Alger: Barzakh, 2013, 88. My translation and emphasis.

77 Ibid., 16. My emphasis.

78 Ibid. 40. My emphasis.

aware of this explicit connection. For the quoted words and sentences I have emphasized with italics, which clarify and underscore this deliberate conflation of Meursault with Camus, were removed from the censored French edition published a year after the original unexpurgated Algerian edition. It appears that censorship was the condition of publication in France.

The back cover of the Algerian edition describes the book as a '"distortion" and "falsification" of Camus's original text', presenting Daoud's work as 'a final act of reparation'.

In a complete contrast, the back cover of the French edition speaks of an adaptation, of a 'counterpoint conceived as homage'. The French readership is flattered. This was only the beginning of a long enterprise of seduction that would very quickly become mutual. Like Camus, who adjusted his texts according to his readership (depending on whether it was pied-noir or metropolitan – as we saw in the case of *The Adulterous Woman*) and according to the times (*Caligula* was revised during the war), Kamel Daoud likewise proves highly sensitive to the French commercial and political context. Paradoxically, through these manouevres, the entire background – what had previously remained unsaid – is brought into relief by the adaptation of Daoud's novel to the French market. For what must remain unstated is this: to be published in France, one must leave Camus off the hook. The critique of *The Stranger* must therefore be softened; Camus must be exonerated in order to secure acceptance from the guardians of respectable opinion.[79]

---

79 *Meursault, contre-enquête* in its French version is less a critique of colonialism in *The Stranger* than a form of sampling, for the novel's true targets are Islam and Algerian nationalism. To illustrate his position, Daoud would eventually go so far as to declare that 'the Islamist does not love life' in the pages of *Le Monde* ('Cologne, lieu de fantasmes', 29 January 2016), and that the decolonizer 'hates movement, alternation, and freedom' ('Quand passent les cigognes', in *Son œil dans ma main*, Marseille: Images Plurielles, 2022), thereby sealing his fate: willingly instrumentalized and destined for Parisian summits. As a result, he became the darling of the French establishment and appeared

But beyond economic interests and individual destinies, Camus and his image are an ideological battleground. To appropriate Camus for the French state amounts to nothing less than rewriting French history.

Camus and Madagascar

In September 2017, a public radio station (France Info) reported that it had been seventy years since a bloodbath had been carried out by the French authorities in Madagascar. In March 1947, the Malagasy population rose up. The insurrection spread across the entire island. As in Sétif and Guelma, the French state massacred tens of thousands of insurgents and Malagasy civilians; some experts estimate the death toll at nearly 100,000. As the radio report notes, these events are rarely mentioned in France, and yet one figure emerges:

> Albert Camus stood almost alone when he wrote in *Combat* on 10 May 1947, 'In Madagascar, we are committing the very acts we once condemned in the Germans.' He went on: 'If today French people hear, without indignation, of the methods that other French people sometimes use against Algerians or

---

regularly on television, won literary prizes, and later was installed as an editorialist at *Le Point* – a weekly owned by the oligarch François Pinault. He was subsequently awarded the Jean-Luc Lagardère Prize for 'Journalist of the Year'; he conducted indulgent interviews with the President of the Republic, and so on.

Daoud also distinguished himself through provocations in which he relayed racist and Islamophobic clichés worthy of the French far-right party Rassemblement National, portraying Arab migrants as a unified mass through a binary, essentialist lens – men and women whose souls, he wrote, 'must … be persuaded to change' (*Le Monde*, ibid.). It should nevertheless be noted that these deliberately provocative statements likely say more about the personal trajectory of a man – his past as an imam, and that of one of his brothers, who left Algeria clandestinely to reach England – than about politics as such (see Adam Shatz, 'Stranger Still', *New York Times Magazine*, 1 April 2015).

Malagasy, it is because they live, unconsciously, in the conviction that we are somehow superior to those peoples, and that the choice of means used to assert that superiority scarcely matters.'[80]

What else did Camus say about the massacres perpetrated by France in Madagascar in May 1947? He first declared that the only reliable ('non-suspect') information at his disposal consisted of reports of 'atrocities' committed by the rebels and of 'certain aspects of the repression'. Once again, as in his article on the bloodbath at Sétif and Guelma, Camus distinguishes between the counter-violence of the colonized ('atrocities') and the violence of the colonists ('repression'). Despite the disparity in the number of victims, despite the context, Camus refuses to choose: 'Rather than hold an opinion, I feel instead an equal repugnance towards both methods.'[81]

Camus therefore hints at the massacres at Sétif and Guelma in his article, euphemizing them and avoiding naming them directly: 'In Algeria … methods of collective repression were used.' What he explicitly refuses to address is 'the heart of the problem', that is, colonialism; for his real subject – the one on which he wishes to dwell – is indeed 'the manner which gives one pause'. Camus is a tactician of colonialism. His article 'The Contagion' is a warning to the authorities: beware of methods that risk unleashing an epidemic of insurrectional plague in our colonies.

Despite his concerns about how the empire should be managed, it is clear that, for Camus, the real enemies are the Malagasy. After comparing certain actions of the French to those of the Germans – a passage triumphantly quoted on France Info – he immediately goes on to compare two enemies of France, the Malagasy resistance and the Nazis, both answerable in law before her:

---

80   Laurent Ribadeau Dumas, '1947: la répression s'abat sur Madagascar, alors colonie française', franceinfo.fr, accessed 12 August 2025.

81   Albert Camus, 'La Contagion', *Combat*, 10 May 1947, reprinted in *Œuvres complètes*, vol. II, 429–31.

Yet the fact remains, clear and hideous as truth itself. In such cases, we are doing what we reproached the Germans for doing. I know full well the explanation that has been offered: *the Malagasy rebels, too, tortured French people. But the cowardice and crimes of the enemy do not excuse our becoming cowardly and criminal in turn. I have not heard that we built crematoria to avenge ourselves on the Nazis.* Until proven otherwise, we opposed them with courts of law. The proof of justice lies in justice that is clear and firm – and it is that justice which should represent France.[82]

This comparison and this defence of colonial justice are unsurprisingly omitted by the state broadcaster. For here the writer's function is to save France's honour; reading this portrait – unrealistic, to say the least – it is easy to imagine a Camus committed to justice for all peoples – an anti-colonialist Camus.

---

82   Camus, 'La Contagion', 430. My emphasis.

Conclusion

Camus, Precursor of Postmodernity

> *A nation that does not colonize is irrevocably destined to socialism.*
>
> – Ernest Renan

Camus was also a precursor. *The Stranger*, both his masterpiece and the most direct expression of his ideological ambiguities, anticipates postmodernity.

Meursault is a man who has lost all enthusiasm for the promises of modernity: work, science, justice, education, love, and bourgeois marriage – all these grand narratives are neutralized in the novel by the radical indifference of its anti-hero. Yet this apparent collapse of values barely conceals the novel's material foundations. The fictional universe of *The Stranger* is shaped by two organizing structures: the labour movement – which grants the pied-noir characters their weekend leisure – and colonial exploitation. As Christiane Chaulet-Achour explains, the murder in the novel gives expression to an implicit rule in French Algeria: in public spaces, the colonized must yield to the colonist on pain of death.

This tableau mirrors postmodernity, a period that sustains its claim to apolitical neutrality by installing figures such as Camus as its guardians. As for Sartre, when he is written about today it is most often to discuss everything *except* his political commitments;[1] *The Words*, his least political text, is frequently

---

1   See, for example, François Noudelmann, *Un tout autre Sartre*, Paris: Gallimard, 2020.

celebrated. He pays a heavy price for his scathing public denunciations of the French Republic's imperial hypocrisy, the most famous of which remains his preface to Fanon's *The Wretched of the Earth*, in which he lashes out at the feeble title of a series of articles by Camus:

> We must first confront this unexpected spectacle: the striptease of our humanism. Here it is, naked, and not pretty: it was nothing but a lying ideology, the exquisite justification of pillage; its tenderness and preciosity sanctioned our aggressions. They cut a fine figure, these non-violent types: neither victims nor executioners! Come on! If you are not victims, when the Government you endorsed, when the Army in which your young brothers served – without hesitation or remorse – undertook a 'genocide', then you are unquestionably executioners.[2]

One of the keys to Camus's current popularity owes much to the way in which, by recasting colonial massacres as expressions of settler despair worthy of compassion, he adopts the double discourse of the colonial left. This runs from Jules Ferry's civilizing mission, through the rhetoric of 'law and order' under François Mitterrand as minister of the interior and of justice during the Algerian War, to the vague homilies of François Hollande, who with studied restraint condemned only 'repression' when referring to the massacre of hundreds of Algerians in Paris in October 1961. These state obfuscations dovetail perfectly with the calculated ambiguity of Camus's political and literary writings.

For a man who styled himself as free from any party or faction, Camus frequented many. He was, in turn, a reformist, a communist, a supporter of the Popular Front, a nihilist, a Munich appeaser, a pacifist, a member of the Resistance, in favour of purges, against them, against de Gaulle, for Mendès France, an anarchist sympathizer, for de Gaulle, against Maurice

---

2   Jean-Paul Sartre, *Préface aux Damnés de la terre*, in *Situations V*, Paris: Gallimard, 1964, 186.

Thorez, opposed to the guillotine (not always), and silent on torture yet in favour of 'the end of imperialisms' while remaining steadfastly opposed to Algerian independence.

These shifts produced the opposite result from what he had intended. He was – and continues to be – appropriated by absolutely everyone. Rather than the declarations of a free man, what we are left with is eclecticism, moralisms, and declamations – so many empty slogans. Or, to put it in the words of Mario Vargas Llosa, who, after having read Camus's *Stockholm Address*, *Letters to a German Friend* and *The Rebel*, spoke of a 'vague and superficial thought':

> commonplaces abound as so many empty formulas; the problems he sets out are always the same dead ends in which he wanders tirelessly, like a prisoner in a tiny cell. These books would be of no interest were it not for his seductive prose, built from short, concise sentences and elusive images.[3]

Decades later, in an entirely different context – far removed from the lucidity of the future Peruvian Nobel laureate in 1962, well before his rightward turn – it is now the unanimism of a certain ideological reception that makes Camus.

There remains the emblematic writer of French social democracy, of the beautiful souls convinced that they have adopted the correct position in contemporary politics. Camus is the figure who allows intellectual comfort, mirroring a France in which, after decades of de-Marxification, every misreading is permitted – where immigration may be endlessly debated, provided colonialism remains unaddressed. To forget Camus as he is currently presented is, at the same time, to cast a more lucid glance on the false pretences of a left that masks its racism and imperialism with a false universalism, and conceals class struggle behind a façade of egalitarianism – a left that has elevated Camus to the status of an icon.

---

3   Mario Vargas Llosa, *Entre Sartre y Camus*, Puerto Rico: Ediciones Huracán, 1981, 17–18. My translation.

Acknowledgements

Belated thanks to the late Pascale Casanova who was the first to suggest this chapter of my dissertation be made into a book well over fifteen years ago. Much gratitude also goes to those who supported the book and what it stands for – sometimes in very different ways – during its tumultuous hexagonal reception and thereafter: Hiba Abid, Miriam Gianni and the wonderful NYPL; Imtinen and Ines Abidi; Mourad Adjabi; Akiko & Cy; Grey Anderson; Yves Ansel; Rachid Arab; Marc Bassets; Mohamed Bedroun; Stella-Magliani-Belkacem and Jean Morisot; Omar Benderra; Vincent Berthelier, Alice de Charentenais and the Séminaire Littéraire des Armes de la Critique; Paul Cassia; Christiane Chaulet-Achour; Claro; John Crutchfield; Roberto Dainnotto and the Institute for Critical Theory; Pierre Daum; Anna Dubosc; Fred Erard; Fethi and Jazair Hope; Hammadi; Pascal Haslé; Teddy Kellogg; the great Hosni Kitouni; Amara Lakhous (for making it happen in Algeria!); Zahia Lameche; Abdel Latreche and Madjid and that voice; Fabien Le Dantec; Jeremy Leeds; Edward Lee-Six; Reslane Lounici; Rym Ouartsi; Christian Phéline; Mabrouck Rachedi; Sarah Samadi; M'hand Smaïl; Djawad Touati; Raymond Thertulien; Enzo Traverso; Nicolas Vieilles-cazes; Arnaud Viviant; Wendy Weiher; Michael Wood; and Gretchen Susi, *last not least*.